The media's watching V
Here's a sampling of our coverage

· ·

"Unflinching, fly-on-the-wall reports... No one gets past company propaganda to the nitty-gritty inside dope better than these guys."
— *Knight-Ridder newspapers*

"Best way to scope out potential employers...Vault has sharp insight into corporate culture and hiring practices."
— *Yahoo! Internet Life*

"Vault has become a de facto Internet outsourcer of the corporate grapevine."
— *Fortune*

"For those hoping to climb the ladder of success, [Vault's] insights are priceless."
— *Money.com*

"Another killer app for the Internet."
— *New York Times*

"If only the company profiles on the top sites would list the 'real' information... Sites such as Vault do this, featuring insights and commentary from employees and industry analysts."
— *The Washington Post*

"A rich repository of information about the world of work."
— *Houston Chronicle*

Use the Internet's
MOST TARGETED
job search tools.

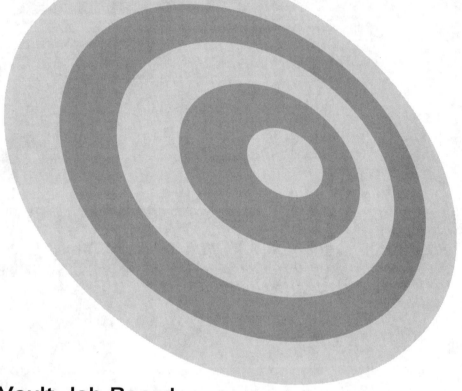

Vault Job Board

Target your search by industry, function, and experience level, and find the job openings that you want.

VaultMatch Resume Database

Vault takes match-making to the next level: post your resume and customize your search by industry, function, experience and more. We'll match job listings with your interests and criteria and e-mail them directly to your in-box.

MARKETING & BRAND MANAGEMENT

VAULT CAREER GUIDE TO

MARKETING & BRAND MANAGEMENT

BY JENNIFER GOODMAN WITH CONTRIBUTING
EDITORS ANDY KANTOR AND JOHN PHILLIPS

For information about permission to reproduce selections from this book, contact Vault Inc., P.O. Box 1772, New York, New York 10011-1772, (212) 366-4212.

Library of Congress CIP Data is available.

ISBN 1-58131-132-X

Printed in the United States of America

Acknowledgments

Vault would like to take the time to acknowledge the assistance and support of Matt Doull, Ahmad Al-Khaled, Lee Black, Eric Ober, Hollinger Capital, Tekbanc, New York City Investment Fund, American Lawyer Media, Globix, Ingram, Hoover's, Glenn Fischer, Mark Hernandez, Ravi Mhatre, Tom Phillips, Carter Weiss, Ken Cron, Ed Somekh, Isidore Mayrock, Zahi Khouri, Sana Sabbagh, Esther Dyson and other Vault investors, as well as our loving families and friends.

Thanks also to Marcy Lerner, Robert Schipano and Ed Shen, and special thanks this year to David Hirschler, Andy Kantor and John Phillips.

Losing sleep over your job search?
Endlessly revising your resume?
Facing a work-related dilemma?

Super-charge your career with Vault's newest career tools: Resume Reviews, Resume Writing, and Career Coaching.

Vault Resume Writing

On average, a hiring manager weeds through 120 resumes for a single job opening. Let our experts write your resume from scratch to make sure it stands out.

- Start with an e-mailed history and 1- to 2-hour phone discussion
- Vault experts will create a first draft
- After feedback and discussion, Vault experts will deliver a final draft, ready for submission

Vault Resume Review

- Submit your resume online
- Receive an in-depth e-mailed critique with suggestions on revisions within TWO BUSINESS DAYS

Vault Career Coach

Whether you are facing a major career change or dealing with a workplace dilemma, our experts can help you make the most educated decision via telephone counseling sessions.

- Sessions are 45-minutes over the telephone

"I have rewritten this resume 12 times and in one review you got to the essence of what I wanted to say!"

– S.G. Atlanta, GA

"It was well worth the price! I have been struggling with this for weeks and in 48 hours you had given me the answers! I now know what I need to change."

– T.H. Pasadena, CA

"I found the coaching so helpful I made three appointments!"

– S.B. New York, NY

For more information go to
www.vault.com/careercoach

VAULT
> the insider career network™

Looking for a new challenge? The Vault Job Board has thousands
of top marketing jobs for all experience levels. Visit www.vault.com.

VAULT   xi

FINAL ANALYSIS 67

APPENDIX 69

MARKETING CASES

Introduction

Are you fascinated by the endless variety of products you pass on your trips down supermarket aisles? Do you like to scrutinize particularly eye-catching cereal boxes or shampoo bottles? Do you watch TV advertisements and think about what type of consumers they are targeting, and how they are accomplishing their goals? Do you see those endless spin-offs of existing products, and think you can come up with better versions?

With an overflow of advertising emanating from ever-forming genres of mass media, and with an economy that allows the masses to increasingly indulge in status symbols, we all live in a branded world. Furthermore, there are people who make handsome livings for thinking like you, or more precisely, for creating and manipulating the branded world in which we live. These cognoscenti are marketers and brand managers. These are the people who devise new products, decide how to package them, how to price them, and most importantly, how to market them. And while Wall Street may yank on our purse strings, and Hollywood may shape our dreams and prurient fantasies, it is the brand managers whose hands guide everything we eat and wear, and influence the way we think about consumption in our society.

Looking for a new challenge? The Vault Job Board has thousands of top marketing jobs for all experience levels. Visit www.vault.com.

VAULT 1

Functional Overview

CHAPTER 1

What is a marketer? The allure of brand management

Marketing encompasses a wide variety of meanings and activities. Some marketing positions are very close to sales, while others set overarching marketing strategy. What marketing positions have in common is the sense of ownership over the product or service, as well as the need to understand customer needs and desires and translate those needs into some kind of marketing communication, advertising campaign or sales effort. The manager of product or service marketing is called the brand manager — he or she is the ruler of that marketing universe.

Careers within the marketing/branding arena are high-profile. The business world is now realizing that strong brands and solid marketing programs drive shareholder value, and that companies can no longer make fundamental strategy decisions without truly understanding how to market a product. Today's business challenges — the quest for company growth, industry consolidation and deregulation, economic webs, and the emergency of new channels and technologies — make marketers even more valuable.

The titles of brand manager, product manager, and to a lesser extent, marketing manager are often used to describe the same function — some companies use one title, others use another. Marketing manager tends to be used in industries other than consumer packaged goods; product manager is often used in tech industries. "Brand management" implies more complete supervision of a product. The typical brand management framework gives a brand "group" or "team" — generally comprised of several assistant brand or assistant marketing managers and one supervising brand manager — responsibility for all matters relevant to their product or products. Whether this responsibility is in fact complete depends somewhat on the size of the company relative to the number of brands it has, the location of the brand group, and most importantly, on the company's attitude toward marketing.

How important is the individual brand manager?

Consider the company to determine the level of brand manager responsibility. The first factor: the size of the company relative to its number of brands. For a company with hundreds of different brands — Nabisco, for example — brand managers, or even assistant brand managers, may have a great deal of power over a specific brand. At companies with a few core products, brand managers will focus on narrower aspects of a brand. As one recently hired assistant brand manager at Coca-Cola comments: "They're not going to take an MBA and say, 'Okay, you're in charge of Sprite.'" Brand managers at such companies will instead be focused on marketing to a particular demographic or geographic group, or perhaps handling one aspect of the product's consumption (plastic bottles, cases of aluminum cans, and so forth).

International brand managers have historically held more sway than managers in the company's home market, but keep in mind that the daily tasks of international brand managers often lean more toward questions of operations, rather than questions of strategy or marketing. ('How much should we produce?' or 'How is our distribution network affecting sales?' rather than 'What do we want our brand identity to be?') International brand management is sometimes split into two positions. Global brand managers are more strategic, concentrating on issues such as protecting brand equity and developing product offerings that can be rolled out into subsidiaries. Local brand managers are more tactical. Local managers focus on executing global plans that are delivered to them, and tweak them for local consumers. Also know that with the increasing trend toward globalization and the truly global presence of certain brands, companies have sought to impose more centralization and tighter controls on the marketing of those brands from country to country. In the past, individual country managers have had more discretion and leeway to make decisions about a brand's packaging, advertising, etc. Now, companies have established tighter guidelines on what can be done with regard to a brand around the world, with the goal of protecting and enhancing the value of the brand and ensuring a consistent product and message worldwide.

Finally, consumer products companies place varying levels of importance on their brand or marketing departments. Some companies, such as the Ford Motor Company, are driven as much by financial analyses of production costs or operations considerations as by marketing. The level of emphasis on finance or operations matters at a firm will influence not only the independence and authority of marketing managers, but also potential marketing career paths. At some companies, marketing is the training ground for general management. At General Mills, marketing is considered so important that employees in other functions who show promise are plucked from their positions and put into the department.

Careers in Marketing

Taking charge of a brand involves tackling many diverse job functions — and different subspecialties. Decide where you'd like your main concentration to lie.

Brand Management

In a typical brand management organizational structure, positions are developed around responsibility for a particular product rather than a specific functional expertise (i.e. you're an assistant brand manager for Cheerios). This structure enables you to be the "master of all trades," acquiring an expertise in areas such as manufacturing, sales, research and development, and communications. In brand management, the marketing function is responsible for key general management decisions such as long-term business strategy, pricing, product development direction and, in some cases, profit and loss responsibility. Brand management offers a terrific way to learn intensively about a particular product category (you could be a recognized expert on tampons!) and to manage the responsibility of running a business and influencing its performance.

The core of brand work is brand strategy. Brand managers must decide how to increase market share, which markets and demographic groups to target, and what types of advertising and special promotions to use. And at the very heart of brand strategy is identifying a product's "brand identity." Brand groups then figure out how to exploit brand strategy, or, in some cases, how to change it. PepsiCo's Mountain Dew has built the drink's popularity among youth as a high-caffeine beverage into a "brand identity" of cutting-edge bravado that has boosted market share, while the Banana Republic chain underwent a transformation from an outdoor adventure store that sold actual army-navy surplus to an upscale, chic clothing store. In both cases, the brands have benefited from a shift in brand identity, and consequently, a shift in their market. Brand identity is normally created and confirmed through traditional print, radio, and TV advertising. Advertising is usually produced by outside agencies, although brand insiders determine the emphasis and target of the advertising.

Looking for a new challenge? The Vault Job Board has thousands of top marketing jobs for all experience levels. Visit www.vault.com.

VAULT   5

Some liken a brand manager to a hub at the center of a hub and spoke system, with the spokes going out to departments like finance, sales, manufacturing, R&D, etc. It is the job of the brand manager to influence the performance of those groups — over whom he or she has no direct authority — in order to optimize the performance of his or her brand or product line.

Advertising

If you enjoy watching commercials more than television programs, then consider the advertising side of marketing. As an account executive, your role is to serve as a liaison between your brand management client and the departments within your agency. Account executives manage the creative production process from beginning to end, from researching what benefits a product offers, to writing the strategy for a typical commercial. Account executives must also handle matters such as briefing the creative department on how to execute the advertising strategies, working with the media department to buy ad time or space, and determining how to spend the marketing budget for advertising. (Will potential consumers be best reached via TV, outdoor billboards, print or radio — or through a general saturation campaign?) Along with managing the creative process, account executives at ad agencies are increasingly becoming strategic experts in utilizing traditional media, digital media, direct marketing and other services.

Direct Marketing

Ever wonder who is responsible for making those coupons you receive in the mail? Or the Saab videotape you've received every two years since you bought your car in 1993? You can thank direct marketers. Direct marketers are masters in one-to-one marketing. Direct marketers assemble databases of individual consumers who fit within their target market, go after them with a personal approach, and manage the production process from strategy inception to out-the-door distribution.

Direct marketers have two main objectives: to stay in touch with their current consumer base and to try and generate more business by finding individuals who fit a target set of criteria but are not currently using their particular product. For instance, if you've ever checked out of the supermarket and got a coupon for Advil after buying a bottle of Tylenol, chances are a direct marketer is trying to convince you to switch brands by offering you a monetary incentive.

It's important to note that direct marketing isn't just through snail mail. It operates in multiple media such as the Web, telemarketing, and in-store promotions. Direct marketers have a powerful new tool in their arsenal — the Internet. Marketers are able to track the online habits and behavior of customers. They can then serve up customized banner advertisements that are much more likely to be relavant to them. Many consumers have agreed to receive promotional offers on certain subjects — marketers can then send them targeted e-mail messages that allow for much easier access to purchase or action (a click on a link, for example) than a conventional mail direct marketing programs.

Affiliate/Property Marketing

If you're working with a major brand company like Nike, Disney, Pepsi, or L'Oreal, chances are you'll do a lot of cross-promotion, or "affiliate marketing." For instance, Nike has marketing relationships with the NBA, NFL, and a variety of individual athletes and athletic teams. Disney has a strong relationship with McDonalds; cute toys from the entertainment company's latest flick are often packaged with McDonalds Happy Meals upon the release of each new movie. L'Oreal works with celebrities like Heather Locklear and sponsors events such as the annual Academy Awards.

Marketers must manage the relationship between any two entities. If Disney wants to promote the cartoon du jour with McDonalds, or Pepsi wants to make sure that all Six Flags theme parks have a Pepsi Ride, then marketers ensure both parties are getting what they need out of the deal and staying true to their own brand image.

Price Marketing/Sales Forecast

Pricing is largely driven by market pressure. Most people, for example, won't pay more than $2.00 for a hamburger in a fast food restaurant. On the other hand, brand managers always have some pricing leeway that can greatly affect market share and profitability. An increase of a nickel in the price of a product sold by the millions can make huge differences in revenue — assuming the price rise doesn't cause equivalent millions less of the products to be sold. Brand managers need to figure out the optimal pricing strategy for their product, though it's not always a case of making the most money. Sometimes it makes more sense to win market share while taking lower profits. How do brand managers justify their prices? Through extensive

Looking for a new challenge? The Vault Job Board has thousands
of top marketing jobs for all experience levels. Visit www.vault.com.

VAULT   7

research. Paper towels, for example, may be much more price-sensitive than a luxury item like engagement rings or smoked salmon.

Brand and marketing managers don't always have free reign over pricing. At some companies, such as those that sell largely through mail order, or those with complex pricing systems, pricing and promotional offers may be limited to what the operational sales system can handle. Explains one marketing manager at a long-distance phone company (an industry with notoriously tangled pricing plans): "It's very easy to offer something to the customer. It's very difficult to implement that in the computer system."

Another large part of the general management duties of brand managers is forecasting product sales. This means not only keeping track of sales trends of one's product, but anticipating responses to marketing campaigns and product launches or changes. The forecasts are used to determine production levels. Once a year, brand groups draw up budgets for their production, advertising and promotion costs, try to convince the finance folks that they absolutely need that amount, get less than they ask for, and then rework their budgets to fit the given budget. As one international brand manager at one of the world's biggest consumer goods companies puts it: "You don't determine the production and then get that budget; you get the budget, and then determine the production."

High-Tech Marketing

Not everyone markets applesauce for a living. Many people choose to enter the world of high-tech marketing because they want to work with products and technologies that reshape and improve the word around us. These marketers feel that they would rather change the way a person interacts with the world in a sophisticated way, rather than spend time understanding what hair color teenagers find most appealing. High tech marketers spend much of their time understanding research and development issues and working on new product launches.

Technology companies like Intel, Dell, and Microsoft have recognized the power of branding and are utilizing traditional marketing tactics more and more. Amazon's extensive marketing campaign in 1998 helped brand that company in the mind of consumers still new to e-commerce as the company to purchase books (and other products) online. Intel became perhaps the first semiconductor company readily identifiable to the public through its heavily branded "bunny people." Marketing in the high tech world will continue to grow in importance over the next decade, as technology companies become more consumer-oriented (see Microsoft's X-Box). Marketing a service or software product versus a more tangible product is a bit different. It may be a bit more challenging to understand how consumers relate to the product. Inventory and distribution issues may be tracked differently.

Market Research

If you are an analytical person who enjoys numbers and analysis, and enjoys tracking consumer behavior, then market research may be the field for you. A product is much more effective when a company understands the consumer it is targeting. That's where market researchers come in. Market researchers employ a variety of different qualitative and quantitative research techniques to understand consumers. Surveys, tracking systems, focus groups, satisfaction monitors, psychographic and demographic models, and trial/repurchase estimations are all methods researchers use to understand how consumers relate to their products. Researchers who find that consumers associate lemon scents with cleanliness, for example, may suggest that cleansers could drive up sales by adding a lemon aroma.

Public Relations

Public relations professionals manage company communications and relations with the outside world. You can work for an internal PR firm (large companies have their own departments that manage the public relations of all of their brands) or you can work for a PR agency and be placed on a brand account. Public relations executives write public releases to local and national publications and develop ideas that will increase the "buzz" surrounding their brand. Some PR firms have excellent reputations for pulling off "stunts" that get their products in the news and increase their brand recognition. Public relations executives may also be forced to defend a brand in the face of public scrutiny — such as the Tylenol brand during the rash of poisonings in the 1980s. While event-driven functions like press releases and stunts are important, perhaps the most important function of a PR professional is to establish strong relationships with media representatives and to persuade them to cover an interesting story about the company they represent.

Marketing Consulting

Although most well-known consulting firms are known for their expertise in general strategy, many consulting firms now hire industry or functional experts that focus on marketing issues. These firms need people with expertise in the areas of branding, market research, continuous relationship marketing, pricing strategy, and business-to-business marketing — they tend to hire people with previous marketing experience and value consultants who have been successful marketing managers and have lived through the full range of business issues from the inside. McKinsey and Monitor are two general strategy firms that have begun to hire marketing specialists. Other boutique marketing consulting firms, such as Kurt Salmon, focus on certain product categories like beverages, healthcare, and retail. All major ad agencies are also attempting to reinvent themselves as marketing partners focused on marketing strategy beyond simple advertising.

MARKETING CASE

Hallmark Cards — Creating a Category

Eighty-six percent of consumers today would rather buy a Hallmark Card than any other card on the market. Hallmark has been able to command this consumer preference by developing additional consumer buying occasions, relating to distinct consumer targets and creating extremely relevant advertising. If you think that holidays such as Valentine's Day, Mother's Day, Father's Day, and Groundhog's Day were created by Hallmark, then you're wrong. But, what Hallmark has created is the perception that you must get a card for your loved ones on all of these occasions. In addition to creating additional buying occasions for their product, Hallmark has done a better job than anyone else at targeting distinct ethnic and racial groups. Since card-giving is so personal, Hallmark created an extensive market research department that probed meaningful messages for Jewish, Hispanic, African American and teenage consumers. As a result, Hallmark has a distinct product line for distinct consumer targets in order to serve them better. Lastly, Hallmark creates advertising that gets right to the heart. The commercials (usually two minutes long in order to paint a story) remind you of the first time you received a Valentine, the bond between sisters and the jitters you felt before asking someone to the prom. If you don't want to rush out and buy a Hallmark Card after seeing one of those vignettes, then you're not human.

Building Your Marketing Foundation

CHAPTER 2

The Marketing Mindset

The best marketers are sensitive to cultural trends. A skilled marketer is a bit of a cultural anthropologist — she loves to watch how people do things, asks why they do the things they do, and creates products and services that can make a person's life easier. Marketers must not only identify cultural trends, but also develop implications of these trends and determine how these implications might alter how a product interacts with and relates to consumers.

Societal trends

The first part of understanding your market is understanding what broad social trends may affect it. Below are some major trends you should be attuned to as a marketer.

- **FAMILY FRAGMENTATION** — Divorce rates remain at high levels. Working mothers with young children are now common. According to the U.S. Census Population Survey, single parent households increased by 27 percent between 1970 and 1994. About half of American children live in homes without their natural fathers. Only 20 percent of American families sit down to dinner together.

- **WORKPLACE/TECHNOLOGICAL DYNAMICS** — Corporate downsizing and displacement are a constant. Part-time and freelance work is more common. More people telecommute. Also, an increasing number of women are taking charge of formerly male-dominated sectors. More and more middle-age workers and middle managers are being "squeezed out" by technological advances. The mouse has replaced the pencil. Science pervades our life and communicating takes on a multitude of forms (e-mail, snail mail, fax, phone, videoconference, express postal services, cell phones, beepers).

- **TRUST NO ONE** — The traditional faith of Americans in the government and other traditional institutions has been broken. People are questioning whether Medicaid and Social Security will survive in this changing economy. A 1996 Luntz Research Survey showed that 74 percent of Americans believe that the U.S. Government is involved in cover-ups and conspiracies. The *X-Files*, a TV series devoted to nutcase conspiracy theories, is a cultural icon. More couples are living together out of wedlock and more people are embracing "spirituality" versus traditional religion.

• **SALAD BOWL** — The term "melting pot" used to refer to the increasing ethnic and religious diversity found in the United States. "Melting pot" implies that distinct cultures are being pushed together and forced to conform to standards. America now publicly embraces diversity and claims that all people can live together peacefully. There is a rise in the number of multi-ethnic celebrities and supermodels, and fashion, culinary, and musical tastes from cultures ranging from China to India to Mexico have made their way into the American mainstream.

Consumer Trends

Societal trends lead to consumer trends — ways in which consumer behavior can be analyzed. Product development is driven by consumer trends. Twenty years ago, no one craved a "sport utility vehicle." Now SUVs are all the rage with posturing motorists tackling the wilds. Recently, consumers have gone gaga over fruit and vanilla scents. Changing customer needs and whims means brand groups must constantly monitor their own market share and product, and the innovations of their competitors.

Product development managers live in horror of missing out on the Next Big Thing. At the same time, sinking company resources into chasing a short-lived fad means career disaster. To help divide the blips from the long-term consumer trends, marketers must pay attention to developments in fields such as nutrition and public safety. Technological innovations, such as the development of a new fabric like Polartec or Tencel, can also effect lasting changes in consumer behavior. Though R&D scientists make these breakthroughs, it is up to brand teams to bring them to the market, devising the types of products to use the new technology, and deciding how to sell the public on the new offering. As with societal trends, we will give some examples of consumer trends.

- **I WANT IT AND I WANT IT NOW!** — Consumers are becoming busier and have less free time. As a result, consumers demand products and services that provide immediate response time. Some of the symptoms of this culture are:

    - Introduction of beepers, cellular phones, e-mail, and instant paging via computer

    - Consumer tendency to use fax machines or e-mail rather than the post office

    - Rising popularity of instant lottery games and the ATM Card

    - Domino's 30-minute pizza delivery guarantee, one-hour film developing, 24-hour supermarket shopping, and a 48-hour home delivery guarantee that has become the norm for retail catalogues such as Victoria's Secret, J. Crew, and L.L. Bean, among others.

- **I CAN'T TAKE IT ANYMORE!** — Because consumers are so busy and are feeling stressed out by the changing workplace and family structure, they risk "burnout." Signs of increasing stress and fatigue are omnipresent and consumers are looking for products and services that will allow them to escape. What products are Americans turning to?

    - Drugs such as Prozac (anti-depressant) have seen a tremendous increase in sales

    - Consumer revitalization with aromatherapy and nutritional herbal supplements (+32 percent since 1996)

    - Nearly 80 percent of Americans now use part of their vacation time to "just stay at home and relax or take care of things around the house" (Research Alert, 9/16/96)

    - The surge in spa retreats, cigar smoking, and premium ice cream all offer small, luxurious temporary escapes for stressed consumers

- **KEEP IT SIMPLE, STUPID!** — Stressed-out consumers are abandoning complexity. Instead, they are embracing lifestyles, relationships, products, and services that save time.

    - The population movement away from urban centers and towards rural areas is occurring three times as fast in the 90's as it was in the 80's

Looking for a new challenge? The Vault Job Board has thousands of top marketing jobs for all experience levels. Visit www.vault.com.

VAULT   13

- The development of Velcro-tied shoes and "point and click" and "remote control-type" products by consumer electronic companies

- The growth in easy-to-make food recipes/food products

- The introduction of business casual in the American work force

• **NOTICE ME! I'M IMPORTANT** — Consumers are now rejecting a "one solution fits all" mentality. How do consumers long to express themselves?

- Create-a-Card concept in Hallmark Stores

- Pick-and-mix candy retailing concepts and salad bars that allow you to "weigh by the pound"

- Growth in tattoos and body piercings

• **TAKE ME BACK IN TIME.** — Appreciation of "yesterday" provides a safe haven for consumers overwhelmed and dissatisfied with how quickly the world is changing. Marketers note:

- Popularity of TV re-runs such as I Love Lucy and The Brady Bunch

- Booming sales of traditional toys like Slinky and Mr. Potato Head

- Resurgence in popularity of cabaret, cigars, and swing music

- The successful relaunch of the VW Beetle

- Return to 70's-style wardrobe and music

• **I WANT TO LIVE FOREVER.** — America's aging population isn't ready to retire gently, and marketers are keen to pick up on this desire:

- Explosion in vitamin sales

- Increase in cosmetic surgery

- Marketing of home fitness equipment

Three Crucial Marketing Frameworks

When you're performing a marketing analysis, you should always be asking the same key questions:

- What are the major problems, opportunities, and threats facing the company?

- What's your strategy to address these issues?

- How much money will you need to make to make this strategy profitable?

- Why did you choose this strategy?

- How will you execute this strategy? What choices do you recommend for the marketing mix and tactics?

The 4 Cs, 5 Ps, and the break-even economic analysis will help you organize these questions and are a great way to begin analyzing a situation.

The 4Cs

The 4 Cs should be used when performing a market assessment and background evaluation of the situation at hand.

Context

- Consider macro-economic factors as well as other external factors (industry, consumer trends)

Company

- Organization's mission/objectives/strategy

- Strengths and weaknesses

- Basis for competitive advantage

- Financial and other performance indicators

- Brand/product specifics

Looking for a new challenge? The Vault Job Board has thousands
of top marketing jobs for all experience levels. Visit www.vault.com.

VAULT   15

Customer Analysis

- Target customer

- Consumer segmentation

- Decision-making process (When do they decide what brand they want to buy — at the store or prior to going shopping?)

- Buying behavior (How often do they buy? What quantities do they buy at one time? Is it an impulse or planned purchase?)

- Latent or unmet consumer needs (Can you own something that no competitor has capitalized on yet?)

Competitor Analysis

- Basis of competition

- Degree of rivalry

- Major players and anticipated new entrants

- Competitor positioning

- Strengths/weaknesses of competitors as well as opportunities and threats

- Company specifics that might affect competition in the future (cost structure, change in focus)

The 5Ps

The 5 Ps should be used when you're ready to recommend a plan of action and create marketing mix specifics.

People

- Market selection

- Customer segmentation

- Estimation of market size

Product

- Positioning

- Product benefits (both tangible and intangible, in other words, functional AND emotional)

- Brand equity

- Packaging

Price

- Recommendations should consider unit cost, perceived value pricing (e.g. premium pricing for prestige)

- Skim vs. penetration pricing

- Price leader vs. price follower

- Role of consumer price promotion

- Elasticity analysis

Place/Distribution

- Channel selection

- Channel power and control (brand/store loyalty)

- Channel margins

- Channel support (financing, training)

Promotion

- Marketing message/motive (awareness, interest level, trial, repurchase, loyalty issues)

- Medium (TV, magazines, billboards)

- Pull and/or push strategy

Looking for a new challenge? The Vault Job Board has thousands of top marketing jobs for all experience levels. Visit www.vault.com.

VAULT   17

Break-even analysis

The break-even analysis should be done to determine:

- Whether a company should enter a new market with a product

- How many units a company needs to sell of a certain product to break even or be profitable

- How much market share a brand will need to make the launch financially successful

- What margins the manufacturers and retailers will need to secure

Example:

Mattel is deciding whether to start manufacturing their Mr. Potato Head Doll in Peru. They hope to sell the doll to local retailers for $23.00. Retailers in this market like to have a 40 percent margin on the goods they sell to customers.

The start-up investment, including all equipment to manufacture the dolls, will total $30,142. The cost of goods sold per doll is $5.25. The annual volume of sales is anticipated to reach 3,800, or a 19 percent share of the Peruvian market. Should Mattel launch Mr. Potato Head in Peru?

Step 1. Break-even volume (in units) = **Fixed Costs**

(Unit selling price — variable cost per unit)

Example:	Fixed Costs	=	$30,142	
	($23 - $5.25)		$17.75	= 1,698 DOLLS
				TO BREAK EVEN ON INVESTMENT

Step 2. Break-even market share = **Break-even Volume (in units)**

Total market size (in units)

Example:	Break-even Volume	=	1,698 dolls (previous analysis)
	Total market sales	=	20,000 dolls (3,800 is 19% of x) = 8.5% MARKET SHARE

Step 3. Unit Contribution = **Unit Selling Price — Variable Cost = Unit Contribution**

Example:	Unit selling price/doll	=	$23.00
	- Variable costs	=	$ 5.25
	Unit Contribution	=	$17.75

Step 4. Total Contribution = **Unit Contribution x Volume Sold = Total contribution to overhead and profit**

Example: Unit Contribution   = $17.75 (previous analysis)

- Volume   =   x 3,800 dolls

$17.75 x 3,800 dolls = $67,450   TOTAL   ANNUAL
CONTRIBUTION

Step 5. Unit Cost (at a given level of volume) = **Variable Cost + (Fixed cost/forecasted unit sales) Unit cost at forecasted sales volume**

Example: Variable Cost   = $5.25

Fixed Cost   = $30,142

Unit Sales   = 3,800 dolls

= $5.25 + ($30,142/3800) = $13.18 IS THE COST PER UNIT AT 3800 DOLLS/YEAR

Step 6. Margin   % Margin = **Selling Price to retailer — unit cost**

(on price) **Selling Price to Retailer**

Example: $23 - $13.18   =   43%

$23

Step 7. Retailer Margin % Margin = **Selling price to consumer — unit cost**

(Reseller)   (on price) **Selling Price to Consumer**

Example: $30 - $23   =   23% A 23% margin is too narrow for

$30   Peruvian retailers (who like to have a 40% margin). Mattel should be wary of launching Mr. Potato Head in Peru.

What is a Brand?

Marketing analysis is primarily concerned with identifying a market, understanding it, and developing a product to fill a need in the market. (There are of course, other logistical details, such as understanding what is required to make the product profitable.)

But a product is just a physical object or service. A brand, on the other hand, is a product that has consistent emotional and function benefits attached to it. Products are interchangeable — a brand builds value. Brands engage the consumer, inspire an emotional reaction, and are consistent in their appearance. On a strategic level, brands can be thought of as a relationship between a company and a customer. On a tactical level, a brand is a consistent message that meets the cusotmer at as many touch points as possible.

You can think of a brand as a "promise" to a consumer. It delivers a consistent tangible and emotional benefit — time and time again. Because of the strong focus on quality control at McDonald's, you can pull off the road and stop into a McDonald's virtually anywhere and expect the food and ambience to be consistent. That's what makes it a strong brand.

What attributes create brands?

Consistent strategy

Products that are constantly changing their strategies and market positions will never hold a consistent place in the consumer's mind. Owning a piece of the consumer's mind makes a brand a brand. When you think of a coffee shop, you now think of Starbucks — that's because Starbucks is a successful brand.

Consistent appearance

What do people think of visually when they think of your brand? Everyone knows Nike's logo — an elegant, high-speed swoosh.

Positioning

Good brands must stand for different things than their category competitors. Volvo cars, for example, are associated with safety, while Porsches stand for sporty speed, and Saturns for value and good customer service.

Connection with target audience

A brand must build an emotional connection with the consumers who use it. The consumer must feel that there are no substitutes in the marketplace. Consumers may choose Pepsi or Coke in a blind taste test — but that "preference" has little to do with the drink they actually buy in the supermarket.

Top 13 ways to revitalize a brand

Despite the fact that product categories are becoming more complex every day and marketing budgets are down, brand managers are constantly feeling pressure to increase sales, profits, and market share. This list is adapted from an article in *Brandweek* and provides excellent examples of how companies improved the marketing of brand name products.

1. *Create new usage occasions.* (Wednesday is Prince Spaghetti Day; Orange juice is not just for breakfast anymore, IHOP breakfast for dinner)

2. *Find customers outside your existing target group.* (The Bank for Kids; Gillette for Her product line; and Pert for Kids shampoo)

3. *Discover a new way of using the product.* (Lipton Recipe Soup Mix; Baking Soda can be used as toothpaste; Jell-O pudding can be used as cake filling; Comet Disinfecting Powder not only cleans surfaces in your house, but also is great to use on old garden tools and old sneakers)

4. *Position your product as the one used by professionals and experts.* (Chapstick and Picabo Street; Tide and its "professional launderettes", Trident and an implied endorsement by dentists)

5. *Tell a compelling story about your product's origins.* (Jack Daniels; Nantucket Nectars; Ben & Jerry's)

6. *Create a jingle that relates to your product's unique feature, or associate your brand with music that carries certain associations.* (Heinz ketchup's "Anticipation"; Wisk's "Ring around the Collar"; Alka Seltzer's "Plop, Plop, Fizz, Fizz", Nissan's use of music by The Who)

(continued...)

Looking for a new challenge? The Vault Job Board has thousands of top marketing jobs for all experience levels. Visit www.vault.com.

VAULT   21

(Top 13 ways to revitalize your brand, cont'd)

7. *Develop a new delivery vehicle or packaging convenience.* (Lysol Toilet Bowl Cleaner's "Angle Neck"; the Colgate "Pump")

8. *Create a character to personify your product, ingredient, or attribute or use celebrity spokespeople* (Post's California Raisins; Kraft's Cheesasaurus; Dow's Scrubbing Bubbles, Dave Thomas for Wendy's, Charles Schwab for Charles Schwab, Michael Jordan for Gatorade)

9. *Use media vehicles in a new way.* (P&G created the "soap opera" to advertise their brands; the "Got Milk" campaign effectively uses mouth-watering billboards; newspapers as a means of distributing product samples)

10. *Look for effective tie-ins/partnerships.* (United Airlines serving Starbucks Coffee; McDonald's distributing Disney toys; Gillette distributing razors at Boston Red Sox baseball games)

11. *Promote your product as benign addiction.* (Lay's "Bet You Can't Eat Just One"; Snackwell's "Won't be able to say no")

12. *Become a reason for family and friends togetherness.* (M&M's Make Friends; Kodak Golden Moments; McDonald's after the big baseball game; "Celebrate the Moments of Your Life" with Folgers)

13. *Market around a cause to generate goodwill.* (American Express donating a portion of every transaction to a charity, Anheuser Busch promotes designated drive programs)

The Basics of Advertising

Understanding marketing strategy and brand-building is the "thinking" behind a complete brand campaign. The second part is the "doing," or the advertising. Having a great marketing strategy is useless without buliding a successful brand and maintaining brand image with consumers.

Here we give you a visual primer on the basics of advertising.

What advertising can do

	Examples
Induce trial If you have a new brand and want people to try it, advertising is a great way to gain awareness of the product.	Viagra, Amazon, Baked Lay's Potato Chips
Intensify usage If you have a product/brand that has lost share/marketing momentum, advertising is a great way to "reintroduce" people to the brand and increase usage patterns.	Milk, V-8, Arm & Hammer
Sustain preference If you already have a strong brand but want to maintain high awareness and usage rates, advertising is a great way to "remind" people of why they love your brand and to build their brand loyalty.	Marlboro, Coca-Cola, Budweiser
Confirm imagery If you manage a brand that has a very distinctive image (expensive, elegant, rebellious), advertising is a great way to cement consumer perception of the brand.	Godiva, Lexus, Absolut, Harley-Davidson

Looking for a new challenge? The Vault Job Board has thousands of top marketing jobs for all experience levels. Visit www.vault.com.

VAULT   23

Change habits Your product may force people to reconsider their current behavior. Advertising can make changing a habit "acceptable" because the consumer learns how to change these behaviors through the advertising.	Cellular phones, microwaveable popcorn, Travelocity as an alternative to travel agents
Build product line acceptance Your brand may actually be composed of several individual products. Some advertisers promote an entire line of products. When advertising uses this approach, they are often hoping that if you currently use one product and are happy with it, then you will be more likely to buy other products within the line. This phenomenon is often called the "halo effect."	Kraft, Sears, Gillette, Microsoft
Break the ice for salespeople If the product or service you are marketing is very "sales intensive," then advertising is a good way to help sell the service benefits of the product. Advertising the benifits of a product and making them well known makes selling that product much easier — as consumers are "pre-sold."	Avon, Cisco, Saturn
Build ambience If your product is striving to own a certain consumer emotion, advertising is a great way to "hammer" that emotion home through creatives uses of music, touching vignettes, etc.	Disney World, McDonald's
Prove performance (via "torture tests") If you say that your product is the best in its category, then you better prove it (sometimes in a test vs. the competition). By showing for example that Tide cleans better than any other detergent, advertising helps to build the performance profile of the brand.	Timex, Jeep, Tide, Motrin

Evaluating an Ad

As you prepare for a marketing career, evaluate advertisements. Here are some questions that you should ask yourself every time you flip on the TV, leaf through a magazine, or tune into the radio.

— What is the objective or goal of this piece of communication?

— Who is the consumer target? Is there more than one target? (i.e. many foods products target both kids and their moms)

— What is the consumer insight or accepted consumer belief that led to the need for this ad.

— What is the message being conveyed? What does the brand promise and what support do they have to confirm that promise? For example, Tylenol might promise effective headache relief BECAUSE they have more pain reliever than any other over the counter medicine.

— How is the message communicated? What creative devices does the ad use (music, special effects)? What is the tone of the ad?

— Is the ad effective? If you are in the target group, does it appeal to you? If you're not in the target group, do you think that it attracts those who are in the target group? Is it memorable? Does it make you want to go out and change your habits?

Looking for a new challenge? The Vault Job Board has thousands of top marketing jobs for all experience levels. Visit www.vault.com.

VAULT   25

What makes an ad effective?

Simple

    Clear

    Specific

    Single-minded

Memorable

    Breaks through the clutter

    Engaging, involving

    Strong brand registration

Persuasive

    Relevant

    Meaningful

    Establishes distinctive point of difference

    Convincing

    Fits with overall business strategy

INCREASED SALES!

What makes an ad ineffective?

Overly complex

    Confusing

    Ambiguous

    Trying to accomplish ten different things

Not Memorable

    Doesn't grab your attention

    Doesn't keep your attention

    Poor brand linkage — Confusion about what brand is being advertised

Not Persuasive

    Not consumer-relevant (no one thinks like that!)

    Not targeted (to new country, ethnic group)

    Doesn't differentiate product from other competitors

    Inconsistent with consumer perceptions of brand

NO/NEGATIVE IMPACT ON SALES!

The Medium is the Message

A large part of developing an advertising campaign is choosing the medium of delivering a message: radio, TV, newspaper, etc. Here's a look at the chief considerations when choosing a medium:

Target audience: The target audience is defined demographically (e.g. age, gender, income, education) and psychographically (mindset, behavior). For example, a target audience for the Jeep Wrangler might be college educated men from 18 to 45 years old, with a household income of over $45,000.

Communication goals: Measurement of how many consumers you are reaching (called "reach") and how often you are reaching them (called "frequency"). (Reach x Frequency = Gross Rating Points)

Geography: Where the advertising will appear. Why advertise suntan lotion in Alaska?

Seasonality/scheduling: Linking the advertising to the product's seasonality or special events. Winter is the prime time for advertising flu medicine. The first half of Febuary is a good time for Hallmark ads. Advertisers may choose to air Rogaine ads (for male hair loss) during sporting events.

Most major marketing companies use a variety of media in their advertising. Not only can this help them reach larger audiences, but each medium can help to reinforce each other. For example, magazine ads can reinforce and deepen a TV message. Billboards located near purchase locations can help remind consumers of brand strengths that may be more fully articulated in TV or radio ads. Radio ads can reinforce jingles initially heard on TV. Internet advertising can provide an avenue for a consumer to immediately check out a product that they may have seen in a magazine ad, but had not explored.

Looking for a new challenge? The Vault Job Board has thousands of top marketing jobs for all experience levels. Visit www.vault.com.

VAULT   27

	Strengths	Weaknesses
TV	• Mass reach • Immediacy • Sight, sound, motion, color • Choice of national and local reach	• High out-of-pocket cost • Transitory • Clutter (lots of competition nearby) • Poor reach of infequent viewers
CABLE TV	• Reach targeted audiences • Low out-of-pocket cost	• Not national coverage
MAGAZINES	• Reach targeted audiences • Compatible editorial • Unit size flexibility • Longer copy • Longer shelf life	• Clutter • Hard to track consumer
NEWS-PAPERS	• Immediate • Newsworthy • Local orientation • Broad coverage	• High out-of-pocket cost • Short life • Clutter • Selective audience
RADIO	• Reach targeted audiences • Frequency • National and local coverage	• Background medium (lots of turning the dial) • Clutter • Limited reach • Lack of sight, motion
INTERNET	• Reach targeted audiences • Low out-of-pocket cost • Quick translation from advertising to browsing (or purchasing)	• Clutter • Narrow reach
OUTDOOR	• Dramatic size • Long life • Geographic flexibility	• High out-of-pocket cost • Can't convey detailed message • Hard to monitor viewers

On the Job

CHAPTER 3

Key Responsibilities and Duties

Marketing and brand managers set the strategic direction of their brand and work with many departments to make sure that the strategy is executed.

• **Product development:** Brand managers work extensively with research and development (R&D) to develop new products — the beloved babies of the brand. Managers must sift through extensive marketing data. Brand managers work with R&D and market research departments to determine what functional benefits a product offers. As a marketing or brand manager, you must always have a detailed knowledge of your products' ingredients, what your product is currently capable of performing, and what future developments can make your product even more desirable to your target consumer.

Marketers interpret data about every aspect of a prospective product — its color, texture, smell, packaging — in order to make the product as appealing to consumers as possible. During product launches, brand managers meet often with R&D scientists to ensure the scientists are moving in the right direction.

(Even at high-tech firms, product development is sometimes led by marketers. Usually known as product managers, these marketers find out what the customers want, and then give specifications to engineers on what to make.)

• **The extension:** More common than the new product is the brand extension, which builds on pre-existing products: a new flavor of granola bar; a smaller-sized bottle of ketchup. Brand extensions serve two main functions. They can expand market share into a new market (Frosted Cheerios goes after those who want sweet cereal), and they can help invigorate a sluggish brand. The promise of something new splashed across packages and TV screens opens marketing avenues for the original brand. Then there are product changes. These can be small additions, in order to revitalize a brand (that's why you have purple horseshoes in your Lucky Charms), but can also involve a complete overhaul of a product. The latter change is a risky one: Even mountains of market research can't prevent egregious misinterpretations of brand identity. While consumers may have preferred New Coke in a blind taste test, they shunned it when it arrived on the scene

Looking for a new challenge? The Vault Job Board has thousands of top marketing jobs for all experience levels. Visit www.vault.com.

VAULT 29

in 1985 — and Coke was forced into an embarrassing withdrawal of the newfangled drink just a year before its 100th anniversary.

• **Strategy development:** Once you understand how your product works and to whom it appeals, you (and your brand management team) must develop a communications strategy that conveys the benefits to appropriate consumers. This requires working extensively with market research to understand your consumer needs and how your product can deliver on them. Once you have created the strategy, you will need to work with your ad agency and PR firm to help communicate this plan.

• **Package design:** It is crucial that the packaging on your product reflects the product strategy you have developed. The packaging must be simple to read, but also stand out amongst the competition on the shelf. What color should the packaging be? Should it be bilingual? Will the package withstand wear and tear? Is the size and location of the handle convenient? Not only is package design concerned with function, but aesthetics can be ultra-important as well, and can be a strong part of a brand's identity (Coke's contour bottle and the Hershey's aluminum wrapper with inserted paper strip are classic examples of packages that have become synonymous with the product). A particularly appealing package design can often drive product sales. And design extends beyond packaging all the way to corporate identity, involving aspects such as marketing materials and display vehicles. The process of package design is identical to that followed during product launches: research and more research, meetings with R&D scientists, and test trials.

• **Market research:** As a marketing manager, you must understand what consumer studies and tracking devices can be used to glean the most information about your product. Whether you conduct focus groups to test the latest product concept, track trial and satisfaction rates for your latest launch, measure market share in a certain market, or assess competitive activity, understanding and executing market research will be a huge part of your job.

• **Trade marketing:** Trade marketing involves marketing to corporations and other organizations rather than consumers. Elements in trade marketing include events such as conventions, merchandising relationships with partners that may involve custome packaging, temporary or permanent displays, promotional overlays, or exclusive promotional pricing, and other marketing programs designed to target corporations and organizations.

- **Sales force management:** Because you know your product's functional and emotional attributes better than anyone else does, it makes sense that you should be the one to educate the sales force. Attending meetings to explain what your sales goals are, and helping to design promotions that will motivate your sales force to hit the pavement are also part of the job.

- **Business forecasts:** Brand managers determine how much of a product you will sell over a certain time period. By doing extensive research on the state of the market, the intensity of competition and how seasonality affects product sales, you will be able to effectively predict market share and profitability. Business forecasting includes margin improvement/cost savings and inventory management.

- **Financial analysis:** Chances are that as a brand manager, you will be given profit and loss responsibility. You will have to create a budget with your team and get it approved by senior management. From this budget, you will determine just how extensive your communications campaign and product development pipeline can be.

- **Promotions:** So, you want to encourage kids to eat twice as much Lucky Charms? Or you want to get more people to buy bottles of Sprite, not cans? Promotions may be the best way to accomplish your goal. For example, you may want to have a coupon made or have a direct mail piece sent to individual consumers' homes. As a brand or marketing manager, you will work with your PR agency and/or internal promotions department to develop a strategy and execute such an event.

- **Advertising:** Whether it's print, TV, radio, Internet, or outdoor advertising, the marketers work with advertisers to create a strategy, execute a commercial, and put it on the air. Advertising may be done in-house or through an outside agency.

- **Customer Relationship Management (CRM):** Getting new customers is only half the battle — the easiest customers to sell to are those who have already used your product. Customer relationship management involves customer service, database marketing, and consumer affairs public relations efforts.

- **Media:** You have an advertising strategy and $15 million to spend on it. What media vehicles do you use and what are your communication goals?

Looking for a new challenge? The Vault Job Board has thousands of top marketing jobs for all experience levels. Visit www.vault.com.

VAULT   31

You'll work with the internal media department as well as the media planning and buying departments at the ad agency to make sure that you develop a media plan that reaches exactly who you want to reach.

- **Pricing:** If we decide to take a 5 percent price cut on Lysol disinfectant spray to celebrate the spring cleaning season, how will that affect our overall sales and profitability? You have a crucial role in determining the price sensitivity of your consumer target and what price point reinforces your brand's positioning in relation to the competition.

- **Manufacturing:** How many boxes of Pampers can you get out the door in a month? How many cases need to be shipped to what parts of the country? If you wanted to switch to a new plastic bottle, how long would that take manufacturing to implement? As a brand manager, you will handle lots of operational questions like these.

A Day in the Life of an Assistant Brand Manager (sort of)

You can often spot the assistant brand manager because they are the ones running around like a chicken with its head cut off. You must learn how to balance your time and prioritize. Here's a look at how your time might be spent:

Responsibilities	% of time per day
Meetings	30%
Analysis/data tracking	30%
Writing memos	30%
Answering management queries	30%
Interfacing with other departments	30%
Actually marketing	Optional

Although this is a humorous take on the day of an ABM (talk about giving 150%), there is some truth to it. Days and weeks will go by where you feel like you've just been pushing paper and trying to stay afloat. It is very easy to get comfortable maintaining the businesses rather than creating new opportunities. Although the role of an ABM is mostly one of maintenance, if you want to be a "star," you must shape your brand, not just maintain it.

A more realistic look at a day in the Life of a Brand Manager

8:30   Get into work. Listen to voice mails. Check e-mails. Print out calendar of today's events. Skim the Markets section of the *Wall Street Journal* to find out what's happening "on the street." Go to the cafeteria and grab breakfast. (Of course, you're only eating products that your company produces or has some relationship with!)

9:00   Meet with market research department to discuss specifics of your latest round of quantitative research. You are trying to understand why people are not repurchasing your product, but you don't feel that the data presented actually answers your questions. You decide that you'll need to design another round of research — but where's the money going to come from?

10:00 Budget meeting to determine how you will be spending 2nd quarter funds. Given the decision to spend more money on research, you might need to cancel an instant redeemable coupon or a local promotion in a poorly performing market.

10:30 You head to the long-awaited product development meeting. Your team has recently discussed reformulating your product to take advantage of new technology. This new technology may raise your product's performance levels, but it will cost more to manufacture and will take some advertising effort (and more money) to explain the changes to the consumer. The group must decide whether these changes are strategically and financially justified. As always, very few people agree. You decide to summarize all the costs and benefits to the project and present the issues to your brand manager at the status meeting you have scheduled for the end of the day.

12:00 A fancy lunch with a *People* magazine salesperson. For months the magazine has tried to convince you that your product should be advertised in *People*. During lunch the represenative explains to you how the publication can effectively reach x percent of your target audience and how it can provide you with the extended reach you need to communicate with potential new users. You leave lunch with a fancy *People* backpack and a headache. Where can I find the money to add *People* to my media plan? Let's ask the media

Looking for a new challenge? The Vault Job Board has thousands of top marketing jobs for all experience levels. Visit www.vault.com.

VAULT   33

department (Note: While lunch with ad reps happens occasionally, the days of most brand managers are packed, without the time to spend schmoozing with ad reps. More often, brand managers, who are very focused on their jobs, grab lunch at a corporate cafeteria and take it back to their desks.)

1:30 Media planning meeting. Because sales of your product have come in slightly under budget, you have been forced to give up 10 percent of your media budget. You now must meet with the media department to determine how to cut media funds without sacrificing your goals (to reach 20 percent of your target group, and to have a continuous presence on TV). Maybe you can cut out two weeks of TV advertising in July when not many people are home anyway. But isn't that your product's peak purchase cycle? Decisions, decisions.

2:30 Time to review changes to the latest advertising campaign. Your ad agency presented a new concept about three weeks ago that needed work. You and your brand manager made comments to the storyboard (a drawing that explains a commercial) and now you are anxious to see what the agency has produced. You review the changes with the agency via conference call and promise to present the new work to your brand manager at your status meeting later in the day.

3:15 Keep the ad agency on the phone and bring in the in-house promotions department. This ad campaign will be introduced into a promotional campaign in the top 20 performing markets in the country. You want to make sure that before you get the promotions people working on a concept, they agree with the agency on the strategy going forward. The following 45 minutes is a creative brainstorming session that offers wonderful possibilities. You promise to type all ideas up and distribute them to the group later in the week.

4:00 Strategy development with sales manager. Your category manager is insisting that all brands work to gain a better presence in supermarkets. You meet with the regional sales manager to understand what types of strategies might work to get better shelf space and more consistent in-store promotions. Once you hear his ideas, you start to price options and see if this is possible within your (reduced) current budget.

5:00 Status meeting with brand manager. You present your proposal for increased research expending as well as the implications of the new product development issue. You also review the latest advertising changes and the changes to the media plan. You aggressively present your data and your opinion and discuss these with your boss. The two of you decide on next steps.

6:00 End of the day. You spend an hour checking the 23 e-mail/voice mail messages you received during the day but failed to return. You go through your "in box" to read any documents relevant to your product. You start to attack all of the work you have to do and promise that tomorrow you'll block out some time to make some progress.

Looking for a new challenge? The Vault Job Board has thousands of top marketing jobs for all experience levels. Visit www.vault.com.

VAULT   35

The Functions of a Brand Manager

Pricing

Media

Manufacturing

Advertising

Product
Development

**Brand
Manager**

Promotions

Strategy
Development

Financials

Package
Design

Business
Forecasting

Market
Research

Pricing

The Traditional Brand Management Career Path

Career Phase	Position	Responsibilities	Skill Development
Career Phase I (Learning Phase)	24-36 months as an assistant brand manager. Title change from assistant to associate brand manager usually between 12-18 months.	Interfacing with publicity, media planning, market research, and other departments. Analyzing market research. Writing memos and presenting plans for brand manager.	Learning the field and making connections are the most important task at this stage of the brand career.
Career Phase II (Doing Phase)	Brand manager of small brand for 12-18 months and then brand manager for bigger brand for 12-24 months	Designing and presenting marketing plans to senior management. Defending your recommendations to senior management re: budget levels, research spending, and media plans. Approving the implementation of local print campaigns and promotions. Training ABM's and writing performance evaluations for those you manage.	Using the skills you've learned to make intelligent strategic decisions that will grow the business is the key at this stage. Managing and mentoring also become important.
Career Phase III (Leveraging Phase)	Category manager handling more than one brand	Developing marketing objectives, strategies, goals, and measures for the division you manage. Approving advertising campaigns and promotions for the brands you handle. Evaluating product development issues and deciding how these new products could or could not fit within the budgetary and strategic constraints of the brand.	Leveraging what you have learned in your variety of assignments to help make major category decisions is an important skill at this stage. Finding new business opportunities and building key relationships with industry experts is also important.

Looking for a new challenge? The Vault Job Board has thousands of top marketing jobs for all experience levels. Visit www.vault.com.

VAULT   37

Lifestyle

There are many reasons brand managers choose marketing as their profession. Many enjoy the intellectual challenge of branding. Others seek a more livable lifestyle in their profession. Here's a look at some of the key characteristics of a career in marketing and brand management.

Hours

When it comes to hours, brand managers generally enjoy more balanced lifestyles than those in other world-conquering industries such investment banking, venture capital, media, and consulting. For one thing, they generally have consistent hours — that is, they don't get calls at 3 a.m. telling them that the Indonesian rupiah is crashing, or that the mayor was just arrested for driving while intoxicated. Although brand managers do travel to consumer research, commercial shoots, and sales meetings, these meetings are planned well in advance. Though deadlines do loom, you usually have a good grasp on when you'll be able to leave the office. Brand hours vary from 9 to 5 p.m. during off-season to 7 a.m. to 10 p.m. during planning season (planning season is usually a three-month period in the middle of the fiscal year when each product team is trying to develop marketing plans and recommendations for the following year).

Of course, hours can intensify during budget-preparing season: one assistant brand manager reports working 60+ hours a week for two or three weeks while preparing an annual plan. "It's usually not that bad, but there are long hours during peak periods," says a marketing manager at a major packaged foods company.

Because many major consumer goods companies are expanding overseas, international assignments often present themselves. According to one insider at a major marketing company: "You must be willing to work overseas for five to eight years minimum." And although brand employees generally don't have to work ultra-long hours, "they want to know you'll stay in the office 24-7 if you have to."

Women

Marketing companies generally offer excellent opportunities for women. "Half of my brand manager counterparts are women, with about the same proportion in junior marketing roles," reports one insider at a company that focuses on cleaning products. Says a marketing insider at another consumer goods company: "A lot of women do part-time when they have families. You see a lot of families here, and women with kids. They do promote family in every way, which is great for women, as you are free to leave and take care of matters when you have to."

Bureaucracy and competition

Not all is blissful in marketing land. Many leading brand companies make life uncomfortable for their marketing employees by instituting up-or-out policies that breed stress and competition. At one company, employees (some of them 10-year veterans) who are not promoted are put on "special assignment" — they are given a phone and a desk and told to find another job. "You do get a lot of help from the manager," says an assistant brand manager at that company. "I don't think you get as much help from your peers." Says one insider at another leading marketing company: "There is something of an up-or-out policy in brand. Either you make your numbers on a fairly consistent basis, or you should start looking for employment elsewhere. And at yet another marketing-led company a source says: "Marketing tends to be more high-strung than finance, with more pressure to perform. I don't want to say there's an 'up-or-out' mentality, but evaluations and bonuses are keyed off brand performance." And even at a company where insiders say there is no real up-or-out pressure, one former marketing employee says "I definitely think there was a lot of politicking going on. There's lots of e-mailing cc'ing your boss so you are always making your boss see what you're doing."

Brand Managing vs. Consulting

In comparison to consulting, brand management allows you to get hands-on job experience at a very early stage. New managers are forced to learn the big picture straightaway. Brand management also gives you a lot of experience in executing and implementing marketing ideas. Consultants are technically hired to survey the situation, write a report, and leave the premises. Marketers are never deemed successful until they actually execute the plan they created. Marketers are also said to have a better lifestyle than I-bankers or consultants. Brand managers travel, but not nearly as much as

Looking for a new challenge? The Vault Job Board has thousands of top marketing jobs for all experience levels. Visit www.vault.com.

VAULT   39

consultants and they are known to have more manageable hours (50-60/week vs. 70-80/week).

However, not everything about marketing is rosy. You are not compensated as well as investment bankers or consultants, and it is hard to buck marketing hierarchy. Many of the big marketing firms require newcomers, to follow a set path of advancement (assistant brand manager for two years, a brand manager for three to four years, etc.), regardless of preformance. If you are a more entrepreneurial person who likes to set your own course, we'd recommend going to a smaller marketing firm or moving to a high-tech firm

Pay and perks

In 1999, the average starting marketing salary for MBA graduates was about $70,000 to $74,000. Pay for marketing managers with MBAs at top brand companies is in the $60,000 to $80,000 range; for undergrads on a marketing management track, it's generally $30,000 to $40,000. These payscales are more impressive when one considers that many of these companies are located in low cost-of-living areas. "Keep in mind that $40,000 [here] is comparable to $70 to $80,000 in San Francisco or New York," one insider at one of those companies says. One brand manager at a company located in a similar locale notes that "[This] is a very livable city on the salary." Brand managers also usually work for large, publicly traded companies that offer potentially lucrative pension plans and profit-sharing bonuses. Says one insider at a consumer goods company, "compensation grows to reward people who stay with [the company]."

Says another at a company with a profit-sharing plan: "It's really skewed in favor of longevity. All you really know is all the folks who have been there for a while go on and on about how much they're getting." In short, one employee at a personal hygiene products company says: "Most of the candidates that we grant offers to are also looking at consulting or investment banking. While both of these fields do compensate more highly, there are significant quality of life issues associated with these career choices." Echoes a contact at another leading brand company: "You'll never be rich, but very comfortable."

The good news is that brand careers are perk-heavy. If you are working on a brand that does a lot of advertising and promotions, you will get tickets to almost every show, concert, and party in your area. For instance, Coca-Cola marketers get to attend every Atlanta Braves game and got to meet the Spice Girls backstage on their national tour. (You can't beat that!) Granted, not all brands are as well-connected, but, if you like cultural events and fine food, it will be hard to find an advertising executive or a magazine representative who is not dying to take you to a new restaurant or the latest show. Chances are you'll get free subscriptions to just about any magazine imaginable and you'll be asked to participate in the events that the magazines sponsor. For instance, how about a spa weekend with *Fitness* magazine or a makeover with *Entertainment Weekly*?

On the financial side of benefits, companies often give brand managers stock options and profit sharing as they advance in their careers.

Training

Another key reason people go into traditional packaged goods brand management is that it is widely viewed as the best training ground for marketing management. Companies recruit brand managers from companies like Procter & Gamble, Colgate-Palmolive, Kraft and Clorox to help them market everything from financial services to software. The consumer packaged goods marketing experience is viewed as the gold standard in terms of people larning a disciplined, well-rounded approach to marketing.

Brand management is also a popular choice among MBAs because it is viewed as one of the key paths to general management. Successful companies are often marketing driven, so marketing has a prominent role in their success. And because brand management is so multi-faceted, with sales, finance, manufacturing, R&D involved, a brand manager develops a broad knowledge base and wide-ranging set of skills that makes him or her well-suited for an eventual role in general management.

Looking for a new challenge? The Vault Job Board has thousands of top marketing jobs for all experience levels. Visit www.vault.com.

VAULT   41

Sears — Brand Repositioning

The opportunity to help a client revamp their image and reenergize their bond with consumers is a rare and exciting one. The launch of "The Softer Side of Sears" campaign in 1994 is an excellent example of how a marketing message and advertising campaign can reposition a retailer successfully in the consumer's eye. By rethinking the demographics of their core consumer (a middle-aged woman buying a range of products vs. a 45-year-old man buying hardware), Sears was able to gain a clear understanding of its brand equity and the opportunities the company had to exploit that equity. As a result, they battled their stodgy culture, broadened their appeal beyond the scope of hardware, and changed consumers' perception of Sears as a hardware store to Sears as a multi-dimensional store that offered something for just about every consumer.

Getting Hired

CHAPTER 4

Qualifications

Most brand managers have MBAs. Companies hiring in these fields are looking for both an analytic mind and broad business exposure — talents MBAs possess in abundance. Students at top business schools can expect to be inundated by a flood of free munchies, soap bars, toys, and other goodies that companies hope will entice them to become marketers for their particular munchies, soap bars, and toys. On the other hand, many companies that hire marketers only recruit at certain schools and may only hire a certain number of new hires a year. .

If you don't have an MBA, you're not completely out of luck. Some companies promote members of other departments into brand management. Insiders at one top packaged foods company say young employees — even some in customer service — considered to have high potential are recruited into the marketing function. At another top food company, a source reports that "there was another woman who went from recipe development straight into marketing." However, says that contact, the marketing department still "requires an MBA, or at least proof that you're working on one." Non-MBAs have a better chance trying to crack into small to mid-size firms.

But at even the most prestigious marketing companies, college graduates can wend their way into management-track marketing positions (although companies often require that these employees eventually get MBAs to advance). Undergraduates may also have an easier time breaking into the field through advertising, public relations, or market research, all of which supply part of the marketing tool kit needed to move on to a career in brand management. However, brand management — when it comes down to it — is a bottom-line business, and whatever function you start in, you better feel comfortable with finance and accounting issues.

There is no classic academic background that leads to a career in marketing. Although many schools offer undergraduate degrees in marketing or communications, it is not necessary to major in these disciplines to get started. (It does, however, make a lot of sense to take a few courses in these fields to show that you have an interest.) Since marketing is brand or consumer understanding, and making business decisions based on a consumer's needs, a candidate with a focus in psychology, sociology, or

Looking for a new challenge? The Vault Job Board has thousands of top marketing jobs for all experience levels. Visit www.vault.com.

VAULT   43

business could be just as qualified. The important thing is that you show a passion for understanding how consumers think and behave.

Is Marketing Right For You?

Not everyone is cut out for life in marketing and brand management. Succeeding in the field requires a very specific set of personality traits. See how well you match up.

Enthusiasm

Although it may be hard to live, breathe and dream of barbecue sauce, a brand manager must have — or develop — a love for the product they are working on, or at least be fascinated by the marketing process. You may personally hate the taste of barbecue sauce, but if you are intrigued with when people use it, how they use it, and what memories are created when they use it, then you do have the required consumer passion. Ultimately, it is this drive toward consumer understanding and how to reach consumers that will make you a great marketer.

Leadership

Marketers must be able to create an environment that encourages risk-taking and innovation. A brand manager must be able to develop a strategic direction and then champion it and communicate it across all cross-functional departments. You must be able to align people behind a common goal and achieve results.

Creativity

You must embrace the philosophy that "no brainstorm is a bad brainstorm." In making products stand out in a crowded field, a brand manager must creatively and effectively develop ideas. You must be able to "walk on the wild side" and develop your sense of humor. Who would have ever thought that the L'eggs Egg would have been such a success? Or that the Trix Rabbit would be an icon for children for generations to come? If you aren't creative or you don't feel comfortable surrounded by creativity, then marketing is not right for you.

Good communication

A brand manager must have excellent oral and written talents. Brand managers constantly lead team meetings and write project proposals that will be reviewed by senior management. Clear, analytical, and persuasive writing and presentation skills are vital.

Teamwork

Teamwork is the most essential skill in marketing. All work is done in teams so it is imperative that you create and participate in an environment that fosters and rewards teamwork. A more senior manager will also be asked to manage people underneath you and representatives from other departments. It is crucial that you learn how to train, mentor, and motivate these people.

Analytical

A brand manager must strive to reach business objectives. In order to accomplish these goals, a brand manager must be able to assess ways to track her business and understand how to grow market share and volume.

Adaptability

The marketing environment is always changing. A typical brand manager is only assigned to any given brand for 12 to 18 months. On Monday you could be ridding the world of mildew stains and then on Tuesday be thrust into the world of insect repellants. Each assignment has distinct business issues and team players. Therefore, it is important to be able to adapt quickly and have a "take charge" attitude.

Risk taking

If you don't like to "rock the boat" once in a while, then marketing may not be the right career choice. Every day new products are introduced in strategic ways that force established brands to "reinvent" themselves, or at least rethink their marketing programs. A brand manager must be able to look at business situations from a variety of perspectives and take acceptable risks. You must feel comfortable making smart business decisions when not all the data is available and when using your intuition is crucial.

Good judgement

Marketing managers must not be swayed by personal biases. For instance, you might adore a particular ad campaign but the consumers in your focus groups hate it. A good brand manager must put her own preferences aside, because attracting consumers is key.

Looking for a new challenge? The Vault Job Board has thousands of top marketing jobs for all experience levels. Visit www.vault.com.

VAULT   45

How to create a winning resume

Make sure that your resume has an emphasis on marketing, no matter what your prior experience may have been. Also, realize that nothing is overlooked on your resume. If you mentioned in the personal section that you love impersonating rock stars, be sure to practice your Bruce Springsteen routine before walking into the interview room. Here are some quick tips to get you started:

- **Get someone who knows absolutely nothing about your prior experience to review your resume to see if it makes sense to them.** Most people fail to realize that they use "industry-speak" that makes sense only to those with a similar background. The simpler and clearer the resume, the better your chances are of getting an interview.

- **Emphasize teamwork, leadership, passion, and creativity.** Many marketing firms believe that if you worked on a team before and you were in previous leadership roles, it is likely that you will continue to grow these attributes. Having a passion for anything translates well in an environment where you must believe in your brand. You may not have been in a "creative field," but if you can prove that you are capable of "out-of-the-box" thinking, then your chances at a marketing career are improved.

- **Scatter marketing terminology throughout your resume regardless of your background.** Words like "cross-functional teams," "customer needs," "strategic direction," "portfolio management," and "communications platform" make you look like a marketer even if you were a banker. But don't overdo it!

- **Focus on results.** If you lead a cross-functional team through a budgetary process, quantify your results. (For example, "I saved the firm $25,000.") This shows that you can succeed when given a task, and that you are action-oriented.

- **Illustrate your love for consumer behavior.** Maybe you majored in psychology or cultural anthropology at your undergrad university. Maybe you were a manufacturer, but your favorite part of the job was understanding how to make things easier for consumers to use. Maybe you were a banker, but really enjoyed understanding why people invested the way they did. Whatever angle you take, make sure that consumer understanding is clearly demonstrated in your resume.

Cover letters that kick butt and take names

Marketer, market thyself! View your cover letter as the one opportunity to sell yourself to a potential employer. Many consultants and bankers will tell you that cover letters don't matter — but in marketing, they mean a lot! If you don't exhibit proper grammar or spelling, your resume will be thrown away. If your letter is too long or unclear, you don't have a chance. Plan on spending many hours on your basic cover letter. Tailoring the letter to specific firms should be easy once you've created the shell. Here are some tips to get you started:

- **Make sure you have the right contact person and spell their name correctly.** If a recruiter's name is Pat, make sure you find out whether Pat is male or female.

- **Send a letter to everyone you meet.** Although there may be an official contact person, it never hurts to send cover letters to everyone you've met during the recruiting process. If you met an employee during a career fair or a company briefing, make sure to send them a cover letter and mention how much you enjoyed meeting them at so-and-so event on so-and-so date. You should also mention that you met these people to the official recruiter that is accepting cover letters.

- **Clearly state how your background positions you to succeed in the job you are applying for.** Don't be embarrassed to sell yourself. You don't want your cover letter to convey that you conquered the world in just a few short years but you do want the recruiter to realize that you are a "star."

- **If you are making a major career change, explain why that experience helped build your skills, and why you now want to make a change.** If you are having a difficult time explaining how an investment banking background will make you wildly proficient at marketing Kraft Macaroni & Cheese, spend some time explaining what skills you got from banking, but also focus on what that particular job lacked (and what marketing has).

- **Demonstrate why you and the firm are a good fit.** For instance a sentence like, "Given Quaker's strengths in ___, ____, and _____ and my passion for ___ and ____, I think we'd be a good match."

Looking for a new challenge? The Vault Job Board has thousands of top marketing jobs for all experience levels. Visit www.vault.com.

V/\ULT   47

- **The cover letter is a supplement to your resume, so don't be redundant.** Pick a few themes that seem to develop out of your resume and have your cover letter spell those out. The reader will toss your resume aside if they find themselves reading resume specifics. Tease them with your cover letter — make them want to flip to the next page.

- **Call to follow up within a few days of mailing your letter.** Many people fail to do this because they fear they will seem too aggressive. I have never heard anyone say, "I didn't hire that person because they showed too much interest in the position we were offering!" If you can't reach the contact to whom you sent the letter, then try calling other people within the firm who you might have met.

Targeted Letters

Here are a few opening paragraphs that really make an impact. They target specific marketing positions, and clearly demonstrate interest in the marketing industry.

For an MBA internship

- "As a first-year student, I have decided to focus my summer internship search on strong marketing and product development programs, which will leverage the skills I developed as a management consultant at X firm. As my section representative for the marketing club, I have been active in using the club to research brand management internship opportunities.

I found X company's brand management internship to be very attractive for its flexibility in allowing interns to work on well-defined projects within an individual brand group while also teaching key skills required of associate marketing managers.

Because I am looking to move from consulting into a general management career, a strong foundation in brand management would offer a challenging and rewarding entry into longer-term career options at X firm."

- "It was a real pleasure meeting you at the House of Blues reception on Thursday, October 23. Our conversation regarding the challenges and opportunities that the brand management division faces has made me even more enthusiastic about pursuing a summer internship with X. Given X's focus on innovation and consumer understanding, and my background in creative marketing, I feel that we would be a perfect fit."

- "I am a first-year student at X school and am pursuing summer internship opportunities in marketing with pharmaceutical companies.

I am particularly interested in X because of its recent restructuring to address the fundamental changes occurring in the health care market. This indicates not only the company's commitment to meeting the shifting needs of the market, but also promises opportunities for employees to assume new responsibilities and help shape the direction of the company. I feel that my consulting skills and experience with the managed care market have prepared me well for the summer position."

Experienced Hire

- "I developed a real passion for understanding consumer needs during my four years at X. As an account supervisor serving the needs of consumer products companies such as Procter & Gamble, General Mills, and Johnson & Johnson, I spent much of my time analyzing market trends and consumer dynamics, and developing creative and innovative strategies that would differentiate our clients' products in the marketplace. I gained broad exposure to a number of marketing functions and learned quickly how to build leadership, analytical, and creative problem-solving skills. My time spent on new product development and international assignments heightened my ability to set the strategic direction of a brand and manage multifunctional teams."

MBA Graduate

- "My three years at X were critical in helping me build a strong foundation in strategic analysis and quantitative techniques for understanding business problems. Nearly all of my engagements

Looking for a new challenge? The Vault Job Board has thousands of top marketing jobs for all experience levels. Visit www.vault.com.

VAULT   49

were strategic assignments which forced me to understand our client's constraints not only from an internal perspective but also in light of changing industry parameters. I was promoted to the associate level while at X, traditionally a post-MBA position, and had the opportunity to lead significant pieces of work with client teams. During my summer internship at X, I focused on improving my ability to work with different functional groups, a prerequisite for new venture projects, and an important skill which can be leveraged with clients.

- "As described in your career presentation, X searches for individuals with initiative, leadership, analytical skills, communication skills, creativity, and the ability to work with others. During my years in public accounting, I developed and displayed all of these general management skills and also gained strong supervisory, time budgeting, and project management experience. My background and enthusiasm provide me with an excellent foundation from which to be a valuable contributor to a brand management team."

Networking

Networking for a job means finding ways to make personal contacts and stand out from the crowd. Networking is also a excellent skill for marketers. Here's how to get started.

First, make sure that you take business cards when the opportunity presents itself and follow-up with a phone call. Also: Attend any company briefings or dinners that you can. Companies do track how often you show up at events and they will feel really guilty not giving you at least an interview after you've attended five events that they have held.

Write personal thank you notes promptly. It doesn't matter whether it's typed, handwritten, or e-mailed — any form will do. A quick note saying that you enjoyed meeting with them and talking about "x topic" will cement you in their mind.

The Headhunting Game

The marketing industry is very tight-knit. There's also a significant amount of employee turnover, which means that marketers have numerous contacts in companies throughout the industry. This strong community creates an excellent networking environment. Headhunters will call you with job openings on your first day of work. It is common for friends within the industry to ask a headhunter to call you to see if you are interested in the position.

A quick word on headhunters: some are very effective, but be careful. By definition, headhunters are more concerned with making money from placing you than they are worried about your long-term career goals. Proceed with caution. Never give a headhunter your resume without finding out exactly how it is to be used. Also, make sure that the headhunter understands your goals and needs, and only calls you when they have a position that might be a good fit.

Although it is smart to be cautious, headhunters are also great people to know. There's nothing wrong with meeting a headhunter for lunch when you are happy in your current job and establishing a relationship. You'll be able to better gauge your marketing worth and the headhunter will call you whenever a promising position comes across their desk.

What Should You Look For in a Marketing Company?

Every job seeker has different needs. These are a few guidelines to help determine whether a particular company is a good fit.

Does it provide a good training ground?

This is important especially if you are new to the marketing field. It will be very hard for you to move ahead if you do not acquire a basic marketing foundation at an early stage. Traditional packaged goods companies such as Procter & Gamble, Clorox, Kraft, and General Mills are known for their extensive and well-regarded training. New brand manager trainees spend days in branding and product positioning seminars and learn the art of media planning, advertising, market mapping, etc. You may not want to start off at

Looking for a new challenge? The Vault Job Board has thousands of top marketing jobs for all experience levels. Visit www.vault.com.

VAULT   51

such a big company (or you may not want to live in Cincinnati). If this is the case, make sure that you are going to a company that offers you the opportunity to meet mentors and offers a firm grounding in marketing.

Does it offer breadth or depth of products?

Since every product faces different business issues, it is important to investigate different product channels. For instance, if your first assignment is on hair care products, you will probably learn a lot about retail channel strategies, fashion trends, and talent sponsorship issues. If you were branding pharmaceuticals, you might have to decide how to how to create relationships with doctors and hospitals, and attempt to determine what types of people use medications and why they use them.

Keep in mind that working in different categories makes you more marketable. It's wise when choosing a company to find one that has a diverse portfolio of brands. On the other hand, a company like Clorox might have fewer brands, but sell them in a very wide variety of markets and to many different audiences.

Will you be able to experiment with different consumer targets and media vehicles?

Just as different product categories can introduce you to a variety of marketing issues, so can distinct consumer targets. For instance, you could go to a company like Coca-Cola or Nike that dominates one particular category but learn a tremendous amount because each product line targets a distinct consumer target. For instance, marketing Coca-Cola to Hispanic Americans would be very different than marketing Surge to teenage boys.

It's important for you to find a category that enables you to learn more about distinct consumer segments. It is also useful to gain broad exposure to media vehicles. Your first assignment might be working on a brand that has a small budget and a pretty focused target, so the brand only uses print advertising. Do your best. That ensures that your next assignment gives you exposure to TV, billboard, public relations, and other types of communication.

Will you have the freedom to move up the ladder at your own pace?

The bigger the company is, the more hierarchical and bureaucratic it is likely to be. Most large marketing firms require marketers to put in a set amount of time before promotion. Although it makes sense that you must master certain skills before you move up the chain of responsibility, make sure that you are evaluated on your contributions, not your tenure. Talk to others who are in the position you are thinking of accepting. If you find that for the past three years, no one has been able to move between assignments, you might want to take this into consideration.

Do you want an international assignment?

Although this may not be a priority for everyone, an international assignment can be extremely valuable to career advancement. You not only get to learn how your brand translates in different cultures, but you also learn more about the overseas operations of your particular firm. In the long run, an international assignment gives you more connections, more credibility, and more leverage. If the company you are considering has international offices, find out how quickly you would undertake an international rotation before you accept the job. You might find out that international assignments are a "carrot" that the firm rarely bestows. Conversely, you might find that the company expects you to go abroad within two years.

Will you get "hands-on" responsibility early?

Don't expect a company to let you make major strategic decisions in your first six months on the job. However, make sure that you are learning about the business, handling profit and loss issues, and are ultimately accountable for product performance. The unstated rule of management is that the bigger the brand you work on, the less involved you will be. For instance, you are more likely to have an impact on business development issues for Lemon Scent Glad Garbage Bags before you'd be able to influence the future of Mountain Dew. If you are working on a company's "baby" or the big money maker, then chances are senior management will be much more involved with all key business decisions. Although it may sound cooler to work on a well-known brand, you might be able to learn more by working on a smaller player at the start of your career. Along with early responsibility, you should also pay attention to training and mentoring opportuntites with the company. Many companies, cognizant of the importance of mentoring and training, offer formalized programs that you should investigate.

Will this lead to a bigger job down the road?

You are the only one that truly understands your long-term goals. Find a job and company that you are passionate about and will help you fulfill those

Looking for a new challenge? The Vault Job Board has thousands
of top marketing jobs for all experience levels. Visit www.vault.com.

V/\ULT   53

goals. If you really want to be an e-commerce expert, then don't worry about the fact that rutabaga.com may not have the best training program. If you really want to establish a career in sports marketing, then push to work on a brand with sports affiliations, like Gatorade. If you want to move into a general management career, then consider working on a larger, more blue-chip brand. Work for companies and on assignments that will give you the skills you need in order to get where you want to be in the long run.

MARKETING CASE

Snackwell's — Creating Consumer Demand

Whoever says public relations can't drive a brand is not familiar with the story of the Snackwell's Cookies launch. Nabisco introduced the line of low fat cookies and crackers in 1994, unaware of just how popular the brand would become.

What ensued was a real-life cookie shortage because consumer demand was so high. Snackwell's decided to make this "consumer frenzy" the center of their communications plan. The created an award-winning advertising campaign that depicted a Snackwell's delivery man being harassed relentlessly by three eager women. The brand also bought huge two-page spreads in national newspapers declaring, "We're sorry we can't make our cookies fast enough for you — but don't worry, they're coming soon!" The campaign not only reassured consumers who were already sold on the brand but also piqued the interest of those who had not yet tried the cookies. When the cookies finally got to the shelf, everyone was waiting for them.

Today, Snackwell's has grown into a $400 million brand. The company is aggressively seeking gaps in the snacking market where Snackwell's can fit consumers' needs for lowfat, tasty snacks. The brand is racing to leverage the brand in as many segments as possible and has already entered the ice cream, frozen novelties, bakery pies, cereal and snack bar categories.

The Interview

CHAPTER 5

The Inquisition

Every company has a different interviewing style. Some companies will give you marketing "cases," and others will focus more on examples of your demonstrated leadership and accomplishments. Many companies will ask detailed questions about your resume. It is worthwhile (if possible) to talk to people who have worked at the company before interviewing to know what kind of questions to prepare for.

General Tips

• *This is your time.* Get across your agenda. You can be passive and let the interviewer control you, or you can proactively mold the interview to illustrate your strengths. Walk into the interview with three or four key selling points and make sure you use them. Take full advantage of questions like "Tell me about yourself." That's your cue to spell out the themes in your life that will make you the best candidate for the job.

• *Be confident. Smile.* Talk slowly and confidently. Shake hands when you enter and exit the room. Personalize your answers by using their name once in a while in the course of conversation. For example, "I was once working on a team, Bill, when we were challenged with the task… "

• *Support all of your key selling points with numerous of examples.* If you walk into an interview with only one example of a leadership experience, teamwork experience, an analytical challenge, and a good and bad advertising campaign, you are totally screwed. Make sure you can fire away with at least four examples of each. Also, make sure that you review them beforehand so that your best three examples of leadership are also your only examples that support teamwork. Have enough experiences to go around.

• *Cooperate with the interviewer.* Although you may be nervous, remember that your interviewer is calling the shots. Be patient and ask the interviewer to clarify if you don't understand the question. Feel free to ask for a little time when thinking about the best way to answer a question.

• *Keep it simple and answer the question.* You want to give your interviewer enough info, but you also don't want to talk for so long that you begin to

Looking for a new challenge? The Vault Job Board has thousands of top marketing jobs for all experience levels. Visit www.vault.com.

VAULT 55

ramble and the interviewer becomes distracted. Try and limit all answers to about a minute — two minutes at the most. If your interviewer wants to hear more, she will ask further questions.

• *Be honest.* Questions like "Where else are you interviewing?" and "How seriously are you considering our position" are often uncomfortable to answer. Rather than limit yourself unnecessarily by exclaiming, "You're my first choice and I would take this job in an instant," explain that you would not be sitting here unless you were interested in the position being offered. Regarding where else you are interviewing, mention what you are looking for in an employer and how their company (and a select group of others) fit those criteria.

• *Practice and be prepared.* Develop answers to questions beforehand and have a friend conduct a mock interview. This will help you vocalize your answers. At the same time, don't practice so much that your answers become too pat. This can give off the impression that you are insincere.

• *Listen for the question behind the question.* If an interviewer asks you "Could you live in X city?" what they are really trying to see is whether or not you are committed for the long haul. If they ask you your immediate goals, they are trying to see if the job you are interviewing for is a good fit. If you think for a minute about what they are trying to determine before you answer the question, you will have a better understanding of how to answer the question.

• *Develop questions to ask your interviewer.* Many interviews are won or lost based on interviewee interest. Make sure you ask a combination of company-specific and industry-specific questions. Remember, people love to talk about themselves. End the interview on a positive note by throwing the spotlight on them.

• *Take risks.* No answer is wrong as long as you can support it with clear and logical explanations and thought.

• *Look the part.* Wear a suit and always bring a fresh resume and a writing pad and pen with you. Don't wear cologne, loud nail polish, or anything else that could distract the interviewer. Your best bet: conservative business dress that shows you take the interview seriously.

What You Can do to Prepare

Preparing for your marketing interviews doesn't have to mean hitting the books and working on break-even analysis questions — it can simply mean watching TV and surfing the Internet. Here are some quick pointers that should help you hone your thinking.

- Look for insight into advertising:

  — Ask yourself why a company creates a particular advertisement

  — Ask yourself why, when, and where you are seeing an ad

  — Look for marketing strategies whenever they appear

- Expand your viewing habits:

  — TV   — Magazines

  — Radio   — Billboards

  — Internet   — Other (Popcorn bags at movies, shopping carts in grocery stores, etc.)

- Think of multiple examples of both good and bad advertisements. Make sure your examples span   product categories and consumer targets.

General and Behavioral Questions

These questions are designed to probe your background, experience, interest in brand management, personality and "fit" with the job or the company. Individual answers, of course, will vary depending on your individual experience. Remember to emphasize strong teamwork, creativity, strong communications skills, and analytical ability. Here are some questions you should be prepared to answer.

- **Walk me through your resume.** Highlight teamwork and analytic ability.

- **Why do you want to work with us?** Make sure you are intimately familiar with the company and its products.

Looking for a new challenge? The Vault Job Board has thousands of top marketing jobs for all experience levels. Visit www.vault.com.

VAULT   57

- **Give me an example(s) of a product that is marketed well or poorly and why.** Here's where you show off all the examples you've collected.

- **What was your favorite product or service launch in the last few years? What did you like about it?** Back up your choice with examples.

- **Give me an example of a situation where you ran into a conflict and how you handled it.** Make sure you handled the conflict successfully.

- **Tell me about a project that challenged your analytical and leadership skills.** You will need to provide at least two, and probably three, examples of leadership.

- **Give me an example in which you managed multiple projects at one time.** Multitasking is a key skill.

- **Give me an example of when you worked as part of team.** Again, have multiple examples of teamwork.

Here are some other common questions:

- **How will this job fit into your career plans?**

- **How did you get results in "x" project (from your resume)?**

- **If you were getting resistance from manufacturing (or sales or the legal department) on meeting a product launch deadline, how would you handle it?**

- **Give me three examples of good and bad advertising and tell me why you consider them to be good or bad.**

- **Do you think image is important? Why?**

- **What gets you really excited about marketing?**

- **Who else are you interviewing with?**

- **What do you know about our company culture?**

- **Give me an example of a time when you had to sell an idea to someone who was not interested. How did you do it?**

- **Describe the ideal position in our firm.**

- Why do you think you are qualified for this position?

- How have you motivated other people over whom you had no authority?

- What is your biggest accomplishment and why do you view it as such?

- What is your greatest success? Your worst failure?

- How would you brand yourself?

- How would you define creativity? Give an example of a time when you demonstrated creativity.

- Why do you want to live in _____?

- Can you excel in an unstructured environment?

- How did you prepare for this interview?

- How would you prepare for a meeting or presentation?

- What are your long-term career goals?

- What do you do for fun?

- What are your strengths and weaknesses?

- How would your friends describe you?

- What would you like me to know most that is not in your resume?

- What did you like most/least about each position you held?

- Why did you choose to attend ___ University? What courses have you liked most? Least? Why?

Wacky questions

Because innovation is one of the most important attributes of successful marketing managers, interviewers occasionally will pose an oddball question. Have fun with these. The interviewer is just trying to see if you have a sense of humor and if you can handle a somewhat stressful situation. There are no real right answers — but the wrong answer is one that is fumbling or defensive. The following are all real questions from marketing interviews.

Looking for a new challenge? The Vault Job Board has thousands of top marketing jobs for all experience levels. Visit www.vault.com.

VAULT   59

• If you were an animal, which one would you be?

• What qualities do you think make someone successful in business?

• If you could create the "perfect" job, what would it be? What are the most important things to you in a job?

• If an M&M could talk, what do you think it would say?

• If you were designing a supermarket, how would you lay it out?

• Do you think Mr. Whipple really believed his customers shouldn't squeeze the Charmin?

Questions to ask

Interviewers usually ask candidates if they have any questions; come prepared with some of these. Doing research on the company in order to ask intelligent questions about business practices is a must. Here are some suggestions.

• What do you think makes your company successful? What does it take for someone to be successful at your company?

• Where would I be in five years if I came to your company?

• What is the culture like at your firm?

• What are the biggest business issues that you deal with on a daily business?

• What else do you need to know about me?

• What do you love/hate about marketing? Your product? Your company?

• A question related to the product, such as "How do you think the fact that so many kids are making their own meals is affecting your cereal business?"

The Case Interview

Interviewers will want to know, first and foremost, whether you have the analytical capability and marketing knowledge to run a brand. Case questions will vary in their breadth or specificity — some may be more geared toward figuring out how an applicant formulates long-term strategy, while others will require candidates to price potential promotions. Interviewers want to hear what questions you might ask, what hypoteses you might create and what plan of action you will suggest.

When answering a case question, you must reason out loud. Take a minute or two to map out the question and to organize it in your mind but then begin a dialogue with them. The 4 Cs and 5 Ps are a great way to ensure that you've touched on all key points. Don't openly refer to the framework, however. Beginning an analysis with "Well, the first 'P' is product" will not impress your interviewer. Use the frameworks without being obvious.

Case strategy questions

- **If you grew Christmas trees, how would you increase your market share?**

This is a typical "how to grow a market" question. Interviewers will be most interested in the questions you ask, the assumptions you make and your intuitive understanding of the market forces at work. Don't worry if you don't know how many Christmas trees are currently sold each year, what percent of people keep them in their homes, etc. The interviewers don't expect you to know this information. The most important thing to do is to take the interviewer through your thought process by thinking aloud. You don't realize how many decisions and assumptions you may be making in your head. Don't do yourself a disservice by not voicing those assumptions during the interview. The best way to answer this type of question is to just brainstorm out loud. Breadth of answers is more important than depth in these types of "wacky" market size questions.

A good place to start would be to brainstorm ways to help the market grow. Could you increase the seasonality of X-mas trees? How would you do this? Perhaps start an ad campaign that would find alternate uses for the trees (like a great Valentine's Day gift). Perhaps you would work with R&D to determine if there is a way to make Christmas trees last longer or

Looking for a new challenge? The Vault Job Board has thousands of top marketing jobs for all experience levels. Visit www.vault.com.

VAULT   61

last in hot weather so that they could also be bought as a "summer plant." Zany answers, but at least you are demonstrating creativity and logic.

Brainstorm for your interviewer.

Could you make trees appeal to a bigger consumer target? Perhaps you could "package" trees in the latest fashion packaging so suddenly, young teenagers really want to buy one. Or, you could make trees "collectible" by selling them in five different colors — maybe people will want to collect a whole set of them.

Could you cut the price? Suggest doing a sensitivity analysis to determine how many people don't buy trees because they are too expensive or how many people would buy trees if the cost was lower.

Could you eliminate any competitive threats? One way to increase market share is to get rid of the competition. Is there any competition now? Are people using plastic trees as a substitute for the real thing? Perhaps you could create an awareness campaign that told consumers about the benefits of having a fresh tree vs. a fake one. If done effectively, this could thwart the competition and build your market share.

Could you make the trees more accessible? This argument is all about distribution. The reason why trees are not selling currently is because there are no outlets that are selling them. If you are not driving down a certain street during a certain time of the year, you might never see Christmas trees being sold. Why not put a tree shop on every corner for the entire month of December, as opposed to just the last two weeks? That should build your market share.

- **Pick a product that you like. Pretend you are the brand manager — how would you create your brand strategy and what would it be?**

What would be the objective of your strategy? What consumer target would you be talking to? What would be the most relevant insight to bait them? How and where would you communicate your strategy?

- **If you were the CEO and thinking of pruning our product line, what would you prune and why?**

Consider what the company brand stands for and which products support that brand equity best. Also, what is the size of the businesses at hand, what is your budget, and what is the competition like? This is your opportunity to demonstrate your research on your prospective employer.

- **If you were the CEO, what would you see as the biggest threats and opportunities to our company?**

Answering this question depends on the industry in which you are interviewing. Think macro. The CEO should not be worried about shelf placement at the 7-11; he is much more concerned with where the consumers are heading and whether his company will be there before the consumers get there. Food companies look at online food vendors like peapod.com with both excitement and vague worry. Cleaning product companies are a bit concerned that women work and don't clean as much, and Internet companies are worried that they will never make any money.

- **You are the brand manager for Wheaties in 1991 when you receive a phone call informing you that Magic Johnson has just been diagnosed with AIDS. The basketball player is about to appear on your cereal box. What do you do?**

Do you have the capacity to separate your own personal feelings from business considerations? As a brand manager, your prime concern is to discourage brand switching and maintain the brand image. Now, you decide if having Magic Johnson on the box would help or hurt your brand. Don't forget about media backlash!

- **You're the brand manager for a product that is rapidly losing sales. You could maintain profitability by increasing the price of your product by 10%. What would you consider before doing this?**

You should only increase your price if you have no other options. The real objective here is to increase revenue. There are a lot of alternate ways to do this. You can create a coupon campaign that might cost in the short term but increase consumer sales in the long run. You could reduce the variable costs. You also must consider the price sensitivity of your customer base. Find out how much money you make off each consumer purchase and determine how many more products you would need to sell to solve your lost sales issue. Then, try to determine the percentage of your consumers who might be unwilling to pay (perhaps the percentage that make under a certain amount per year or the percentage that tends to switch among

Looking for a new challenge? The Vault Job Board has thousands of top marketing jobs for all experience levels. Visit www.vault.com.

VAULT   63

brands). Will the lost sales from these consumers exceed the increase in sales you'll receive for increasing your margin?

- **You're the brand manager on Tylenol and your product is threatened by the influx of private label (generic) products. You have two options: (1) to introduce your own private label brand or (2) to have Tylenol compete with private label. What would you do and what issues would you grapple with before making your decision?**

Introducing a private label brand will take away from your main brand's shelf space. It also creates the potential for cannibalization and splinters your manufacturing capabilities. You could heighten your brand equity and engage in smart professional endorsements to differentiate yourself from competitors. (What parent doesn't trust Tylenol for their kids?) On the other hand, someone's going to produce generics anyway. It may be worthwhile to get into the generic drug market.

- **A new product is being introduced into the marketplace. What would you do to make sure that it gets a voice in the marketplace?**

People — Who is your product aimed at and what sector of the market does this target represent? Are you going to pick a product that doesn't have mass appeal? Then you'll need a niche strategy. What are the habits and practices of the product audience? Do they have expensive tastes? Do they have consistent shopping habits or opinions that affect product positioning?

Product — How will your product be positioned and what tangible and intangible benefits will it stand for? What type of packaging, and communications campaign will help you to convey these benefits? What will the product look like? Feel like? Taste like? Ideally, what brand equity will the product gain over time? Think about the brand character of the product. Will it be tough and mean, or soft and sweet? Will it be a hero or a confidante?

Price — How will you price the product? For instance, if you decided to position your product as a "tool that everyone needs," then your price better be one that almost everyone can afford. What will your pricing strategy be? Will you appeal to everyone, or will you start expensive and then lower your costs as you build your market? What type of price promotions will you create? Do you want an everyday low price, or do you want to have a three month period where the price is 25 percent off the original cost?

Place/Distribution — Where will this product be sold? Do you want to be very selective about where you sell it or do you want to "hit people over the head with it" wherever they are? How will the product be placed on the shelf? What products will surround it?

Promotion — How are you going to communicate your product and its attributes to the public? Do you want a huge PR campaign or would you prefer to just advertise on Monday night football? How much money will you spend relative to your competition? Will you focus on having retailers push it through the channel or will you rely on "pull" tactics to create a market?

- **You're a brand manager for a product that has many different line extensions. How do you decide when and where to introduce an additional extension?**

Make sure you have an excellent understanding of what the brand stands for, who is using it, how often they are using it and why and when they are using it. Then, you can decide whether a new line extension fits those factors or if you could afford to make a stretch within the brand portfolio.

- **You're the brand manager on Gatorade. You receive a phone call from a sales rep in Tulsa, OK. She tells you that a competitive product has just been spotted. You have never heard of this product before, but it is being manufactured by your main competitor. The sports drink costs less than yours and has already been granted prime shelf spacing. What do you do right away? In the next few days? In the next month?**

You should be upset that you never heard about this earlier. (Where is competitive intelligence when you need them?) Start by asking very detail-oriented questions so you can start to formulate your own strategy for this brand. What's the price point? What's the brand name? What does the packaging look like? Who does it look like they are targeting? How long has it been in the store? Over the next few days, you should find out if this is a national rollout or just a test market. Is there advertising? If so, what is it saying, where is it playing and how much money is being spent on it? You should begin to set up tracking studies that measure awareness and repurchase of the new brand and get market research involved quickly. Once you see how it is doing, you can determine whether more aggressive, strategic steps need to be taken.

Looking for a new challenge? The Vault Job Board has thousands of top marketing jobs for all experience levels. Visit www.vault.com.

VAULT 65

MARKETING CASE

Saturn — Building a sustainable brand

In the fragmented automobile industry, it is extremely difficult for a car to establish a distinctive, sustainable position. Saturn has been able to do just this by rethinking the game and creating an integrated communications plan that enforces the idea that Saturn is "A different kind of company. A different kind of car." Specifically Saturn did this by:

- Breaking ties with parent company General Motors and developing a "start-up" feel with a unique culture and team-based organizational design.

- Building an emotional attachment with the brand by selling the company and its culture, rather than functional product benefits.

- Revamping the retail program, so price haggling didn't exist and sales representatives were rewarded in based on establishing consumer relations rather than sales.

- Creating promotions that strengthen the relationship between Saturn and their customers. One example is the annual Saturn homecoming where satisfied Saturn owners gather together at Saturn's headquarters for a barbecue.

Today, Saturn is one of the strongest brands in the U.S. It is the 10th-highest selling brand out of over 200 car brand names and loyalty measures indicate that a higher percentage of Saturn users than any other car users would repurchase a Saturn the next time they are in the market to buy a car.

Final Analysis

An early career in marketing will give you exposure to a variety of different product categories. You may find that down the road you want to specialize in an area you were exposed to during one of your rotations. For instance, if you really loved learning about the facets of the health care industry while you worked on the Tylenol account, you may decide to move into a more specialized health care career. If you loved working on sports promotions with PowerBar, then perhaps working for a sports agency is your next career move. Marketing gives you skills that will be valuable in almost any field.

Whatever you decide, you'll find brand management and marketing an interesting way to start a career.

Looking for a new challenge? The Vault Job Board has thousands of top marketing jobs for all experience levels. Visit www.vault.com.

VAULT   67

Losing sleep over your job search?
Endlessly revising your resume?
Facing a work-related dilemma?

Super-charge your career with Vault's newest career tools: Resume Reviews, Resume Writing, and Career Coaching.

Vault Resume Writing

On average, a hiring manager weeds through 120 resumes for a single job opening. Let our experts write your resume from scratch to make sure it stands out.

- Start with an e-mailed history and 1- to 2-hour phone discussion
- Vault experts will create a first draft
- After feedback and discussion, Vault experts will deliver a final draft, ready for submission

Vault Resume Review

- Submit your resume online
- Receive an in-depth e-mailed critique with suggestions on revisions within TWO BUSINESS DAYS

Vault Career Coach

Whether you are facing a major career change or dealing with a workplace dilemma, our experts can help you make the most educated decision via telephone counseling sessions.

- Sessions are 45-minutes over the telephone

For more information go to
www.vault.com/careercoach

V\ULT
> the insider career network™

Appendix

Marketing Jargon/Buzzwords

It's important to realize the distinction between general marketing vocabulary and specific category jargon. For instance, if you decide to work in pharmaceuticals, you'll quickly learn that "OTC' means over the counter. If you become a beverage wrangler, you'll be a whiz at distinguishing a Non-CSD (carbonated soft drinks) from the real thing. This lingo can all be learned on the job. The following are generic marketing terms that you should definitely be familiar with in order to understand what marketers consider before they act.

Brand Equity: The added value that is brand. The reason why you are more likely to buy Tide detergent than a random store brand.

Brand Extension: Use of a popular brand name for a new product entry in another product category or media. Examples: Starbucks ice cream, Oreo's cereal, Lifesavers ice pops.

Brand Recognition: Stage of brand acceptance at which the consumer is aware of the existence of a brand, but does not necessarily prefer it to competing brands. For example, 99 percent of people in the United States recognize the brand Kodak, but they do not all necessarily prefer it.

Brand Preference: Stage at which the consumer will select one brand over competing offerings based on previous experience. You always use Secret deodorant, because you've bought it a few times, it works in hot weather and you like the scent.

Break-even Analysis: Pricing technique used to determine the number of products that must be sold at a specified price in order to generate enough revenue to cover costs. If it costs $x to manufacture, distribute and market a certain type of sunglasses, how much $ will the company need to charge to make sure they are not losing $ on the deal.

Cannibalizing: When products take sales from other brands in the same line, it's called cannibalization. If a new, lemon-scented Ty-D Bowl is marketed, will its sales be generated from consumers who have never purchased a Ty-D-Bowl product or will the new line extension get business only from loyal users, therefore, hurting the

Looking for a new challenge? The Vault Job Board has thousands of top marketing jobs for all experience levels. Visit www.vault.com.

V/\ULT   69

base Ty-D- Bowl business? Is it a good idea to put your entire magazine online if it means that computer users just read it online and don't buy it? At the end of the day, you want more people using your product rather than just a reshuffling of current users.

Concept Testing: Measuring consumer attitudes and perceptions of a product idea prior to the product's actual development. When a company has a novel idea — to create a chewing gum that tastes like green tea, for example — they must conduct research before production.

Elasticity: Measure of the responsiveness of purchasers and suppliers to a change in price. Will people still buy a Jeep Cherokee if it suddenly costs $10,000 more? If the answer is "yes", then the market is elastic, if the answer is "no"; further analysis is required to determine the elasticity of the car consumer.

Everyday Low Pricing (EDLP): Pricing strategy-using prices that are consistently lower than those of competitors. Procter & Gamble developed this strategy to be even more competitive in certain channels. You can accomplish this by cutting back on trade promotions and putting the money saved into lowering the cost of the product.

Focus Group Interview: Information-gathering procedure in marketing research that typically brings together a small group individuals to discuss a given subject. If I'm creating a new type of Hanes Pantyhose for very tall women, I want to talk to female consumers that fit this description and who have bought pantyhose in the last few weeks.

Line Extension: New product that is closely related to other products in the firm's existing line. Examples include caffeine-free Diet Pepsi, Gillette Shaving Gel, Frosted Cheerios, and so on.

Loss Leader: Product priced at less than cost to attract customers to stores in the hope that they will buy other merchandise at regular prices.

A great example is the disposable razor blade. They sell for mere pennies and companies don't make much money from them. But Gillette hopes that you buy a Gilette, gel or aftershave to accompany your purchase or trade up to a reusable razor.

Market Segmentation: Process of dividing the total market into relatively homogenous groups.

Customer-Based: Dividing a market into homogenous groups on the basis of buyers' specifications.

Demographic: Dividing a population into homogenous groups based on characteristics such as age, sex and income level. If I'm selling Sprite, I want to target males ages 12-25.

Psychographic: on the basis of behavioral and lifestyle profiles. If I'm selling Palm Pilots, I want to attract people with are "on the go" and care about organizing their life

Penetration Pricing Strategy: Pricing strategy that uses a relatively low entry price to secure market acceptance. If you don't know if the product will be a success (you could be the first company to create such a product), you don't charge a lot of money so those consumers will be more likely to try your product. As your product gains acceptance, you may be able to raise the price.

Point-of-Purchase Advertising: Display or other promotion located near the site of the actual buying decision. Think of Hershey's Easter promotions at the checkout counters of supermarkets.

Product Positioning: Consumer's perception of a product's attributes, uses, quality and advantages and disadvantages. Products within the same category can be positioned very differently (Mercedes vs. Saturn).

Pulling Strategy: Promotional effort to stimulate consumer demand of a product — literally "pulling" the product through the marketing channel. Directed at the end user. Examples include coupons and advertising.

Pushing Strategy: Promotional effort to stimulate selling of a good or service — literally "pushing" it through the marketing channel. Examples include trade discounts or in-store displays.

Relationship Marketing: An organization's attempt to develop long-term, cost-effective links with individual consumers for mutual benefit. Remember the Coke Card promotion? Every time you bought a Coke, you received discounts towards lots of other services like video rentals, free CD's etc. What you may not have realized is that when you used your card, The Coca-Cola Company was tracking your preferences and habits in an effort to understand you better.

Looking for a new challenge? The Vault Job Board has thousands of top marketing jobs for all experience levels. Visit www.vault.com.

VAULT   71

Skimming Pricing Strategy: Pricing strategy that uses a high entry price relative to competitors' offerings. If you want to establish a prestige, elitist positioning, this is the way to go. Some brand categories that use this approach are automobiles, cosmetics and alcoholic beverages.

Target Market: Group of people toward whom a firm markets its good, services or ideas with a strategy designed to satisfy their specific needs and preferences. For example, a target market may be men between the ages of 18 and 45 who make over $25,000 a year and enjoy watching football.

Recommended Reading

Aaker, David A. *Building Strong Brands.* **New York: Free Press, 1996.** Discover the value of a brand as a strategic asset and a company's primary source of competitive advantage. Uses real brand building cases from Saturn, GE, Kodak, and others to demonstrate how the best brand managers create brand equity.

Arnold, David. *The Handbook of Brand Management.* **Reading, MA: Addison-Wesley Pub. Co., 1993.** A complete resource on managing brand names, the most powerful strategy in marketing.

Bayne, Kim. *The Internet Marketing Plan: A Practical Handbook for Creating, Implementing and Assessing Your Online Presence.* **New York: J. Wiley & Sons, 1997.** This book provides a marketing plan geared toward e-commerce and covers the middle ground between marketing and Web technology.

Carter, David M. *Keeping Score: An Inside Look at Sports Marketing.* **Grants Pass, OR: Oasis Press, 1996.**
Keeping Score explores the multibillion-dollar relationship between Corporate America and the sports industry. Packed with fact-filled case studies, this book reveals the strategies that work for the superstars of sports marketing.

Dupont, Luc. *1001 Advertising Tips.* **Ste. Foy, Quebec: White Rock Pub., 1995.** A step-by-step guide to create advertising that sells. Using dozens of examples of advertising campaigns and marketing strategies, it offers you the insight, tools and techniques you need to market any product or service.

Hatch, Denny and Don Jackson. *2,239 Tested Secrets for Direct Marketing Success.* **Lincolnwood, IL: NTC Business Books, 1998.** A collection of the accumulated wisdom, maxims, rules, discoveries, revelations, standards, principles, canons, code of 20th century direct marketing

Hill, Sam and Glenn Rifkin. *Radical Marketing: From Harvard to Harley, Lessons from Ten That Broke the Rules and Made It Big.* **New York: HarperBusiness, 1999.** In *Radical Marketing*, Hill and Rifkin examine unorthodox companies like Virgin Atlantic, Samuel Adams beer and analyze how their radical market practices have made them wildly successful.

McDonald, William J. *Cases in Strategic Marketing Management: An Integrated Approach.* **Upper Saddle River, NJ: Prentice Hall, 1998.** Designed to help readers

Looking for a new challenge? The Vault Job Board has thousands of top marketing jobs for all experience levels. Visit www.vault.com.

VAULT   73

gain an appreciation for the types of issues in marketing strategy management and develop the analytical and thinking skills necessary to make good decisions in real-world marketing situations.

Murphy, John M. (Ed.). *Branding: A Key Marketing Tool.* **New York: McGraw-Hill, 1987.** This handbook offers techniques for developing brand strategies, managing brands, and maximizing their value. It describes how package designers have come to call themselves "brand identity designers"; how accountants determine whether or not brands should be put on balance sheets; and how corporate finance specialists strive to understand brands and their strong presence in mergers and acquisitions.

Ries, Al, and Jack Trout. *The 22 Immutable Laws of Marketing: Violate Them at Your Own Risk.* **New York: HarperBusiness, 1993.** This book offers the definitive set of 22 innovative laws for understanding and succeeding in the international marketplace.

Adweek Client/Brand Directory. **New York: Adweek, 1998.** Alphabetical listing of 6,000 advertising agencies, public relations firms, and media buying services. Arranged by parent/holding company, and by geographic region. Directory information including functional capabilities, product/service specialties.

Beverage Marketing Directory. Provides company and organization information on beverage industries such as carbonated soft drinks, coffee, bottled water, beer, wine and spirits.

Brands and Their Companies. **Detroit: Gale Research, 1990.** Provides basic information on over 306,000 consumer brands and the 62,000 manufacturers/distributors responsible for them.

Exclusive Brands Sourcebook. Gives an overview of the international private label industry, including grocery and drugstores.

The Official Guide to the American Marketplace. **Ithaca, NY: New Strategist Publications & Consulting, 1992.** Charts on trends in education, health, income, labor force, living arrangements, population, ethnicity, spending and wealth.

Sports Market Place. **Princeton, NJ: Sportsguide, 1984.** Extensive directory of sports companies and organizations, including professional leagues and teams, sports organizations, publications, arenas, stadiums, museums, retailers, sports sponsors, and marketers.

Standard Directory of Advertisers. **New York: National Register Pub. Co., 1998. ("The Red Book").** Known as "The Red Book," this directory profiles of 8,100 national and international advertising agencies and public relations firms. Indexed by company and geographic location. Each profile lists addresses, key accounts and key executive information.

Journals/Publications

• Adweek

• Journal of American Marketing Association

• Brandweek

• American Demographics

• Advertising Age's Business Marketing

• Journal of Consumer Marketing

• Mediaweek

• Sales & Marketing Management

Looking for a new challenge? The Vault Job Board has thousands
of top marketing jobs for all experience levels. Visit www.vault.com.

VAULT   75

VΛULT

About the Author

Jennifer Goodman: Jennifer began her career in marketing at the age of 5, developing creative ways to sell her mother's wormy vegetables from the family garden. Since then, the bulk of her marketing experience has been in the field of advertising. Goodman spent four years at Saatchi & Saatchi Advertising Worldwide where she supervised accounts for clients such as Procter & Gamble, Johnson & Johnson and General Mills. During business school at Harvard Business School, Goodman was President of the marketing club and also spent a summer interning in the Consumer Marketing department of The Coca-Cola Company. She is currently a Marketing Specialist at the consulting firm, McKinsey & Company and is a graduate of Duke University (1993) and Harvard Business School (1999).

Contribtuing Editors

John Phillips: John is the Senior Vice President of Marketing and Operations at Konica Photo Imaging, a systems solution provider for the imaging industry, with an emphasis on consumer products, retail processing systems, and digital products and services. Prior to Konica, John held marketing management positions in packaged goods (Colgate-Palmolive Co.), entertainment (Sony Wonder) and media (SPACE.com). He graduated from Stanford University (BA) and New York University (MBA).

Andy Kantor: Andy has a consulting practice specializing in branding and marketing strategy, based in Scarsdale, New York. Previously, he was a co-founder and Vice President of Marketing at TradeOut.com, and spent 10 years in marketing and brand management at Colgate-Palmolive and Lehn & Fink Products. He received an MBA from the Kellogg School at Northwestern University, a JD from Georgetown University and a BS from Cornell University.

Coca-Cola acquires
Mad River Traders Inc.
5/11/01

Classic Communications to
borrow $75 million in senior
bank debt from CSFB and
Brera Capital Partners. 5/10/01

Procter & Gamble
is turned down in $4-4.5 billion
bid for Clairol. 5/11/01

Kraft Foods hopes to
raise as much
as $8.7 billion in
an IPO. 5/2/01

Gavitec GmbH received
an undisclosed amount
of investment capital
from Gold-Zack AG. 5/10/01

Multiplex Inc. landed
$105 million from several
top investment banks,
including JP Morgan. 5/10/01

Zhone Technologies
withdrew its
$345 million IPO. 5/8/01

US Timberlands receives
$106 buyout offer from senior
management. 5/14/01

Imperial Tobacco buys 75%
stake in Tobaccor. 4/2/01

Facing bankruptcy due to its more
than $1.5 billion in debt, Teligent will lay
off 38% of its workforce. 5/14/01

AB Barrandov a.s. for
sale for $33.3 million.
MGM, Paramount possibly
interested. 5/14/01

Veronis Suhler buys
Phillips Business Information
and Hart Publishing from
Phillips International
for over $100 million. 10/4/00

FINALLY, A DAILY PAPER FOR THE OBSESSED. FINAL

Use the Internet's
MOST TARGETED
job search tools.

Vault Job Board

Target your search by industry, function, and experience level, and find the job openings that you want.

VaultMatch Resume Database

Vault takes match-making to the next level: post your resume and customize your search by industry, function, experience and more. We'll match job listings with your interests and criteria and e-mail them directly to your in-box.